BRIGADIER GENERAL DANIEL DAVIS
and the War of 1812

The DESTINY of the
TWO SWORDS

Michael A. Ponzio

Michael A. Ponzio

Copyright © 2022 Michael A. Ponzio
Trinacria Publishing Company
BISAC: Nonfiction / History / North America
All rights reserved.
ISBN: 978-1-7349723-4-4

Brigadier General Daniel Davis and the War of 1812

ATTRIBUTIONS AND APPRECATIONS

Betty Neracker Davis for her long hours researching the family genealogy.
Lynne Belluscio, Director of the LeRoy Historical Society, for her devoted work preserving LeRoy history.
Franklin Davis- LeRoy, New York, for his valuable recollections.
Chopper Davis as the caretaker of Brigadier General Davis's battle sword.
Anne Davis Ponzio for editing and enhancing this book.
Nancy Soesbee for editing and proofreading.

Cover attribution: The painting (circa 1840) by E. C. Watmoug, depicts the British storming the Northeast Bastion of Fort Erie during their failed assault on August 14, 1814. According to historian Crisfield Johnson, in his *Centennial history of Erie County, New York:* "General Davis bravely mounted a parapet near Battery No.2, at the head of his men," in a sortie from Fort Erie, making the scene fitting for this book.
PD-US-expired. (Public domain-copyright expired) This work is in the public domain in its country of origin and other countries and areas where the copyright term is the author's life plus 100 years or fewer.

Photograph of Ganson's Tavern, Chapter XII: From the collection of the LeRoy Historical Society. Director, Lynne Belluscio.
Maps attributions: Those marked: PD-US-expired are also works in the public domain in its country of origin and other countries and areas where the copyright term is the author's life plus 100 years or fewer. All other maps were created by Michael A. Ponzio and are copyrighted along with this document.

Michael A. Ponzio

Contents

CHAPTER I: Daniel is Born 1776 7

CHAPTER II: July 1776 17

CHAPTER III: British Raid 1779 23

CHAPTER IV: Genesee Fever 1799 31

CHAPTER V: Move to New York 1800 39

CHAPTER VI: 1800-1804 Ganson's Settlement 49

CHAPTER VII: 1805-1806 63

CHAPTER VIII: 1807-1810 71

CHAPTER IX: The War of 1812 Begins 81

CHAPTER X: 1813 89

CHAPTER XI: Battle of Buffalo, December 1813 97

CHAPTER XII: Niagara Frontier, Summer 1814 107

CHAPTER XIII: Muster of the 6th Brigade 119

CHAPTER XIV: The Militia Prepares 129

CHAPTER XV: The Sortie from Fort Erie 135

CHAPTER XVI: The War Ends 145

CHAPTER XVII: The Destiny of the Two Swords 151

BIBLIOGRAPHY 167

Michael A. Ponzio

Brigadier General Daniel Davis and the War of 1812

CHAPTER I: Daniel is Born 1776

Daniel Davis was born on February 23, 1776, in Killingworth, Connecticut, a prosperous village, the home of hardworking and self-sufficient farmers. He would have likely been born in a wood frame house, which had replaced the original log cabin of his great-grandfather, Solomon Davis, Sr. His surname Davis presumes that his family (Solomon Sr. or his father) immigrated from Wales. Davis[1] is a patronym, meaning son of David, and St. David is the patron saint of Wales. "By 1776, about 85% of the white population in the British colonies was of English, Irish, Scottish, or Welsh descent, with 9% of German origin and 4% Dutch." [2]

Daniel joined his older brother, James Jr., born two years earlier. His mother, Hannah Davis, would have had access to the best care available during his birth. Yankee women were just as hardworking as their husbands. "Despite excessive childbearing, they performed feats the mere thought of which would stagger their modern sisters. In [mid-18th century] Windham, Connecticut, Hannah Bradford cared for the town sick for many

---

[1] The Welsh word for David is Dafydd. Pronounced dah-vith in Welsh, becoming, Anglicized to Davis, *"Davis/Davies/David"*, Background.
[2] *"The Growth of the Colonies"*, 3.

years, and is reported to have taught the first male doctor of the community much of his medical lore." [3]

Mrs. Davis's helpers during childbirth, doing duty as midwives, could have been descendants of the early settlers of Killingworth: Daniel Buel, Joseph Griswold, Nathaniel Parmelee, Ebenezer Hull, or Theophilus Redfield.[4] The families may have been close friends with the Davises in Killingworth because historical records show their descendants emigrated to LeRoy, New York,[5] circa 1800, along with Daniel's family. Called "go-outers," many Yankee farmers moved to western New York after the Revolutionary War.

Daniel Davis was born into a theocratic community dominated by the Congregational Church. The Puritans who had originally settled the colonies in Massachusetts and Connecticut had been persecuted for their religious beliefs in Europe. But after coming to America in the early 17th century and establishing the Congregational Church, they fined, expelled, imprisoned, or executed anyone not Puritan. The Congregational Church forced the people in Massachusetts and Connecticut to pay taxes to support the religion and the residents were subject to criminal laws based on the Scriptures.

In 1634, when the Puritans arrested Roger Williams for heresy, he escaped and founded the neighboring colony of Rhode Island, which became a refuge for Quakers, Jews, Baptists, and others from persecution. Roger Williams established the separation of church and state in Rhode Island and no taxes were required to be paid to any religious group. Daniel Davis was eight years old living in Killingworth when "in 1784, Connecticut passed a law so the public would no longer be

---

[3] Bridenbaugh, "*The New England Town: A Way of Life*", 28.
[4] "*First Settlers of the Second Society*", 1.
[5] The proper pronunciation of LeRoy – based on the family for whom the town is named – is "luh roy", Belluscio, *June 8, 1812-2012, "Our Bicentennial"*.

taxed to support the Congregational Church and ensured religious freedom, but only if they were of a Christian sect. Non-Christians were still taxed to support the established church."[6]

By the late 17th century, the success of the earlier pioneer generations had created a secure standard of living for the yeoman farmers. "Every white man who wasn't indentured or criminally bonded had enough land to support a family."[7] Fisheries, water mills, and other industries thrived. The people's devotion, however, was now split between commerce and religion because farmers were producing a small surplus to make life more comfortable.

The Puritans' complete domination in New England had slipped and membership had decreased. As a result, the Congregational Church became more tolerant. Well before Daniel Davis's birth, an English law in 1682 forbade corporal punishment for dissenters. Another reason for the church's softening was the passing of the English Toleration Act of 1689, granting freedom of worship, but only to Trinitarian Protestants.

In the early 1700s, inspired by the rationalism of the "Age of Enlightenment," many people were turning to Deism, Unitarianism, or atheism, and church membership was decreasing. Puritan ministers called for a revival which triggered "The Great Awakening," an evangelistic movement which occurred in England and America. Beginning in the 1730s, preachers, some of them itinerant, held outdoor revivals, with crowds in the thousands. It was common for participants to display great enthusiasm and emotions, and many reported visions and mystical experiences.

Because of the evangelistic movement, the Congregational Church lost followers. "From 1740 to 1776, the percent of

---

[6] "*The Importance of Being Puritan: Church and State in Colonial Connecticut*", 10.
[7] "The Growth of the Colonies", 3.

churches that were Congregational dropped from 34 percent to 21 percent of the churches in America."[8] Even with these changes, the Congregational Church remained the established church in Killingworth when Daniel Davis was born.

The Congregationalists practiced infant baptism, so it is likely that Daniel Davis was baptized soon after his birth. "Rev. William Seward, pastor of the Second Ecclesiastical Society of Killingworth from 1738 to 1782, had performed the marriage ceremony for Daniel's father, James Davis, Sr., and his mother, Hannah Norton, on June 6, 1774. Rev. Seward had also conducted the marriage ceremony for Daniel's grandfather and grandmother, Solomon Jr. Davis and Sybil Griswould, on 14 Jan 1747." [9] Undoubtedly, Reverend Seward baptized Daniel.

The ritual would have been at the Congregational Meetinghouse, as described in a record on the founding of the society, on "a high flat piece of land about 50 rods north of the new bridge over the Bare-Swamp brook."[10] Congregationalists called their places of worship meetinghouses, refraining from using the word church, because it was "popish."

"Children were always carried to the meeting-house for baptism the first Sunday after birth, even in the most bitter weather."[11] The morning of the Sunday service in February, it would certainly have been cold, and the Davis family could have woken up after the evening before, having pulled their mattresses out of the single bedroom to sleep near their fireplace.

What would the morning of Daniel's christening have been like? Daniel's mother, Hannah, would likely have cooked their usual breakfast, "hasty pudding," corn mush, in a black iron pot, hanging on a metal rod she used to swing over the coals in the

---

[8] Noll, America's God: From Jonathan Edwards to Abraham Lincoln, 162.
[9] Bailey, "Early Connecticut Marriages Church of Killingworth".
[10] Lentz, *"History of The Congregational Church in Killingworth"*, 1.
[11] Earle, *"The Sabbath in Puritan New England"*, 32.

fireplace. It was an important day in Daniel's life, and perhaps to two year old brother James Jr's. delight, their mother might have added to the pudding the maple syrup that she had been saving for a special occasion.

Daniel's parents were likely dressed in the same garments they had worn at their wedding, church services, and special events. As did most New Englander farm wives, Hannah used homegrown flax to make their clothes for the warmer seasons, but today they wore wool clothes, the socks, mittens, and cloaks, she made from their own sheep's wool, the "church clothes" bartered in New Haven for surplus cider they produced.[12] James Sr. probably wore stockings, knee breeches, waistcoat, and cloak of wool, all dyed black. He would have brought along his tri-cornered hat, which he would put on for the service, but on the hike to the meetinghouse he would wear his winter montero, a wool stocking cap with ear flaps.

Hannah definitely would have swaddled baby Daniel in warm layers, covering his head with a wool bobbin tied under his chin. She certainly would have dressed Daniel's two year old brother James Jr. in layers of undergarments, socks, and a gown. It would be another year before he would be "breeched," for the reason that boys of the era did not wear pants until they were three or older. He likely wore a montero cap with flaps over his ears. James Jr. would have donned a wool cloak with a hood as well.

Colonial women wore knee-length shifts as undergarments, over which a "jump," a stiffened waistcoat, with laces at the front (unlike a corset) so a woman could put the garment on herself.

---

[12] Jenkins, Edward H., *A History of Connecticut Agriculture*, 44. President Stiles of Yale College enumerates among the wonderful orderings of divine Providence which conspire towards the establishing of the independence of America, "Heaven has led us to the successful experiment on corn stalks from whence it is probable may be made an abundant supply of molasses and rum for this whole continent." Cider was a common beverage in the family and was not by any means a spiritless drink.

Hannah would have pulled on wool stockings and two petticoats for the winter cold, then donned an ankle-length gown. Indigo was a preferred color because it was pleasing but would have been dark enough to match her social class and conservative morals of the time. For her final layer of clothing, perhaps she added a "blue and white checked apron, [the style and pattern] ubiquitous in the Connecticut Valley."[13] As farmers' wives did, she would have fixed her hair in a bun, covered it with a felt mob cap (encircled with ruffles), put on her wool cloak, and pulled up the hood. Her mob cap would still conceal her hair inside the church, although during a cold February service, she would most likely keep her hood up because most Congregational meetinghouses were not heated. Various congregations had tried using stoves, fireplaces, braziers for foot warmers, and even dogs at meetinghouses around New England but halted their use after several meetinghouses burned down or because unruly canines disrupted the sermons. Heat was not provided in the Killingworth meetinghouse either.

The meetinghouse would have been within walking distance of the farms in Killingworth. There were several buildings at the site, the largest being the newest meetinghouse, a robust structure with unpainted clapboard siding, 58 feet long and 38 feet wide. The other structures were the former meetinghouse which had been converted into the town hall and the rectory, the pastor's residence. During the time of Solomon Davis, Sr., baby Daniel's great-grandfather, Sunday service attendance was mandatory, and fines were imposed for those congregation members who were absent. Times had changed by 1776 such that ". . . the church [had become] a social rather than a religious institution. Theological emphasis may have been strong at first [in the early colonies], but after the embers of the Great

---

[13] Miller, *Clothing and Consumers in Rural New England, 1760-1810". The Needle's Eye: "Women and Work in the Age of Revolution.",* 25.

Awakening died down, about 1750, it is probable that the average New England man would rather have wet his whistle with a gill of rum than sweeten his mouth with a morsel of Calvin."[14]

James Sr. would have safely banked the fire by pushing the coals against the back of the brick fireplace and covering them with ashes. The Davis family would have donned mittens and scarves. The two-wheeled cart would be useless on the slippery roads, so they would use the toboggan.[15] Perhaps James Sr. pulled them on the toboggan himself, rather than harness a horse. It was not overly difficult and kept him warm as well. Besides, it was unlikely there would be a place or way to take care of the animal during the service.

Public christenings were customary in the Congregational Church. When Daniel Davis was born, he had at least three uncles, one aunt, and five second cousins on his father's side living in Killingworth. Along with Hannah's family, they would have been at his baptism. Neighbors and friends observing Daniel's baptism would likely have included families with the surnames of Buel, Griswold, Parmelee, Hull, and Redfield, whose descendants 25 years later joined the Davises' migration to LeRoy in Genesee County, New York. The Wilcoxes, Kelseys, and Halls were also living in Killingworth in 1776 and may have been at the meetinghouse that day. Members of their families also moved in the late 18th century to Bergen, also in Genesee County, only eight miles from LeRoy.

---

[14] Bridenbaugh, "*The New England Town: A Way of Life*", 32.
[15] Bills, Joe, "*The Camden Toboggan Chute*", 4. Before Europeans arrived, natives of the northern North America used toboggans to transport people and goods across the snow. The word *toboggan* likely originates from the Mi'kmaq (*tobâkun*) word for "sled." Toboggans were sometimes pulled by snow dogs, but most often by a man or woman wearing a chest harness. Early European settlers adopted toboggans for transport, but soon realized that they had recreational value as well.

At the meetinghouse, the men would have entered through one side door and women the other. The pastor, deacons, and prominent men would have entered through the center door, called the "door of honor."[16] The men and women, even those married, sat in separate sections across the center aisle from each other. Family pew boxes were provided for couples with children. Those of high social standing were seated in the front pews closest to the pulpit. Perhaps families with the surnames of Buel, Nettleton, and Parmalee sat in these pews, being descended from the first European settlers of Killingworth. Boys older than ten sat on the steps or near the raised pulpit under the pastor's and the assembly's watchful eyes.

Although the 16th century Puritans immersed infants during baptism, the Congregational Church in New England had little tolerance for dipping, especially for infants in the cold climate. In 1642 a pastor at Plymouth was removed from his position for insisting to immerse newly born, even in the cold winter months. Instead, water was most likely sprinkled or poured upon baby Daniel Davis. Congregationalist churches were simple, so the Killingworth meetinghouse did not have a baptism font. The sacrament would have been performed with a bowl of water. Most likely the worshippers would have seen their collective breaths rise as white clouds in the frigid meetinghouse and in extremely cold times, a layer of ice would have to be broken to reach the baptismal water.

Assuming children are born with a given temperament, baby Daniel probably did not cry out in the chilly setting when Reverend Seward christened him. Hannah may have believed it was a sign the Holy Spirit was entering her son. James Sr. might have sensed it as a premonition that Daniel would grow to be strong and fearless.

---

[16] Horn, "History of the First Congregational Church of Hamilton Meetinghouses", 3.

Brigadier General Daniel Davis and the War of 1812

Michael A. Ponzio

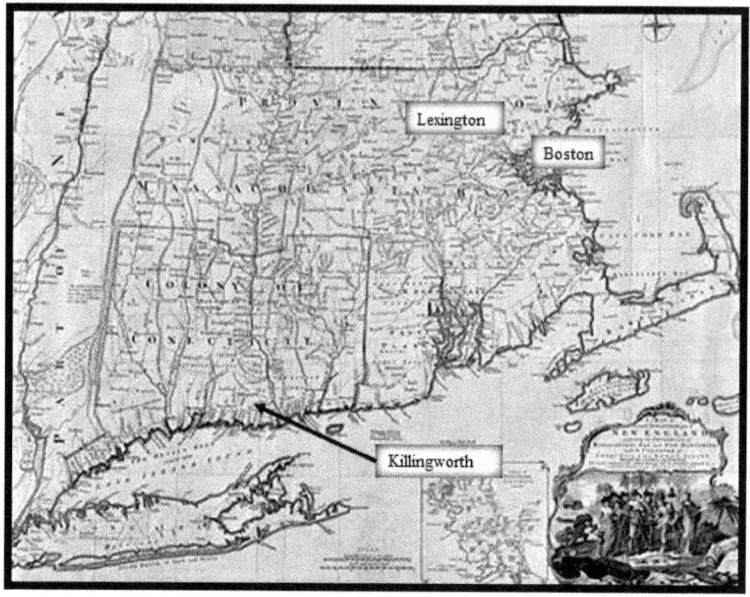

PD-US-expired. This work is in the public domain in its country of origin and other countries and areas where the copyright term is the author's life plus 100 years or fewer.

CHAPTER II: July 1776

In Daniel's infancy his mother would likely have allowed him to crawl, in contrast to the Puritan colonists generations before, who had not let their babies scramble on all fours, equating it to "bestial" actions. At most other times Daniel would have been in his wooden cradle or in his mother's arms nursing.

"Nursing in public seemed to be a non-issue in colonial America. Our foremothers were expected to maintain a busy household, which included feeding the baby, and breastfeeding in the market or other public areas was not a cause for uproar. At that time, breastfeeding was the only way to feed a baby, either by the natural mother or a wet-nurse. The Puritans believed breasts were created for the nourishment of children and strongly encouraged women to nurse their own babies. Breastfeeding in public was commonplace for colonial women because they lived in a society that supported breastfeeding." [17]

Both the old time Puritans and the evolved Yankees of 1776 encouraged their children to walk as early as possible. At five

---

[17] Mays, Women in Early America: Struggle, Survival, and Freedom in a New World.

months, Daniel might have inherited a wooden "go-cart,"[18] a baby walker, from his older brother James Jr. Likely, being self-sufficient in most things, their father would have made it. The walkers gave mothers freedom to work around the house, sewing clothes, making candles or soap, or cooking. The upper ring of the walker held the baby securely erect, and the larger base ring kept him an arm's reach from touching dangerous objects. In the neighboring colony of New York where many descendants of the colonists of New Netherland still spoke Dutch, the mothers called the walkers "loopwagens."

James Sr. would certainly have started this July morning of 1776 with a stiff draught of cider. He had pressed the cider from apples grown in his orchard. Perhaps because it was the summer, he would have had time to hurry off to the local tavern to garner news of the war. During the spring planting and the fall harvesting, colonial farmers worked from the time they "can see" in the morning to the time they "can't see" in the evening, using every daylight hour, but during the summer, their time was more flexible, clearing land, repairing farm tools, or resuming the annual project stacking stone walls at the property lines.[19] Preparing land for cultivation in the rocky landscape of Connecticut produced plenty of stones for the walls and new stones appeared, unceasingly working their way to the surface.

---

[18] *Babywalkers,* When your child is five months old, provided you follow my directions, you may put it into a go-cart...after it is in, tie the cart to the leg of a table or a chair; continue it thus for a fortnight, that it may feel its feet properly...I have [had] one made with a flag to it, to encourage the child to stand upright... Sarah Brown, A letter to a lady on the Mode of conducting herself during pregnancy - also on the management of the infant, 1777.

[19] De Melker, "*Debunking the myth of summer vacation's origins*", Kids in rural, agricultural areas were most needed in the spring, when most crops had to be planted, and in the fall, when crops were harvested and sold. Historically, many attended school in the summer when there was comparatively less need for them on the farm.

Brigadier General Daniel Davis and the War of 1812

Daniel might not have noticed his father leave as he was thoroughly occupied "walking" in his "go-cart" to celebrate his six month birthday in July 1776. Toys weren't usually store bought, so James Jr. may have clacked a pair of wooden spoons together, delighting in the noise, accompanying the "thwack-thwack" of Hannah's loom as she wove a linen shirt. The colonials typically spun their own thread, using fibers from their sheep or flax. The weaving looms required extra space, so the Davises, like many New Englanders, may have built a "loom room" for this reason.

How would James Sr. have stayed informed of events outside of Killingworth? Travelers spread news from tavern to tavern, but these "public houses" could have had copies of the *Connecticut Courant*,[20] a newspaper which had been published weekly in Hartford since 1764. In small rural communities, taverns did extra duty as post offices and "post riders carried mail and newspapers to rural areas with considerable frequency."[21] The entire Declaration of Independence was printed on the second page of the July 15, 1776, edition of the *Connecticut Courant*. The literacy rate among male citizens of New England in 1776 was 80%, so Daniel's father would likely have read that on July 4th Congress had declared the colonies as the free nation of the unanimous thirteen United States of America.

The first battles of the Revolution in neighboring Massachusetts a year earlier may have unnerved the Davises along with the people of Connecticut. The independent-minded Yankee farmers, ready at all times to defend their home and township, were not as keen when summoned to fight for other communities. But on April 18, 1775, after Paul Revere's ride to warn the patriots the British were headed toward Lexington and Concord, towns across New England, including Killingworth,

---
[20] *"The Oldest US Newspaper in Continuous Publication"* The Connecticut, 1.
[21] Bridenbaugh, *"The New England Town: A Way of Life"*, 38.

sent reinforcements to Massachusetts. The "list of men who marched from the Connecticut towns for the relief of Boston for the Lexington Alarm of April 1775"[22] included the names of fifty-three men from Killingworth. Private Peter Davis, twenty-one year old first cousin to Daniel's father, was among the militiamen who answered the call to arms and rushed north. The Americans chased the British back to Boston. The short campaign complete, the men of the Killingworth and other militias returned home within twenty days and commenced planting for the spring. General George Washington's Continental Army besieged the British for almost a year, until March 1776, when they drove the "lobsters," [23] redcoats, out of Boston. With New England rid of the British, the fighting shifted to the Carolinas, but there were rumors the British fleet in Halifax was going to attack New York City.

---

[22] Record of service of Connecticut men in the War of the Revolution, 15.
[23] Bell, "*British Soldiers Weren't Called Lobsterbacks*" [in the American Revolution], Oxford English Dictionary, "lobster" has been used since 1643 as a slang term for English soldiers with red uniforms. The first documented use of "lobsterback" was in 1812 in the newspaper The Tickler of Philadelphia.

Brigadier General Daniel Davis and the War of 1812

Michael A. Ponzio

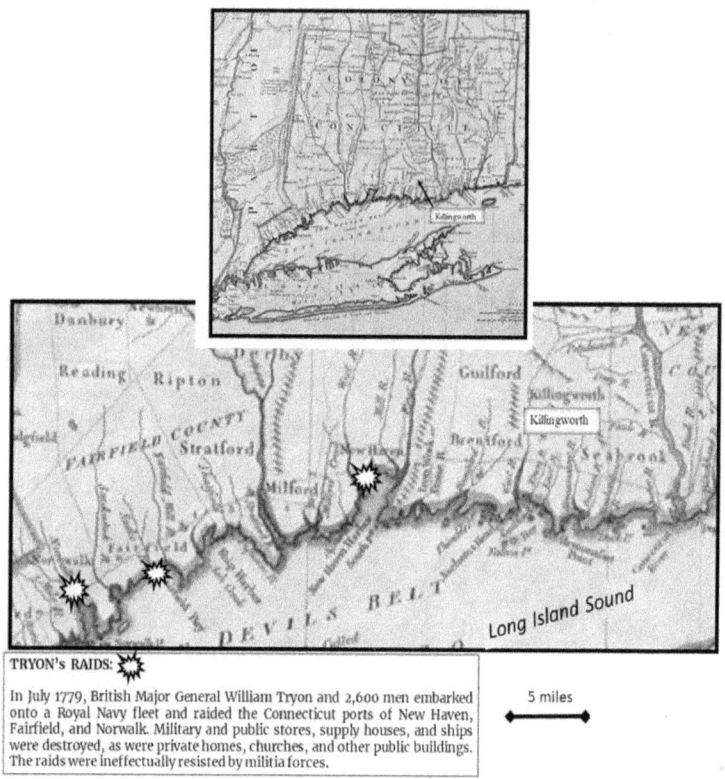

TRYON's RAIDS:

In July 1779, British Major General William Tryon and 2,600 men embarked onto a Royal Navy fleet and raided the Connecticut ports of New Haven, Fairfield, and Norwalk. Military and public stores, supply houses, and ships were destroyed, as were private homes, churches, and other public buildings. The raids were ineffectually resisted by militia forces.

5 miles

PD-US-expired. This work is in the public domain in its country of origin and other countries and areas where the copyright term is the author's life plus 100 years or fewer.

CHAPTER III: British Raid 1779

Except for New York City, which had been occupied by the British Army since September 1776, the young country's largest cities held Independence Day celebrations on Monday, July 5, in 1779, because July 4 had landed on a Sunday. Perhaps the farmers of Killingworth had planned a celebration at the meetinghouse, but Daniel's brother, James Jr., would still have to do his chores in the morning. Typical work for a five-year-old would have been weeding the vegetable garden or husking maize, "Indian corn." Likely Daniel would have imitated his older brother, with Hannah watching both of them while she held Daniel's sister Lydia, only six days old. Being summer, James Sr. may have been working on the endless task of building stone walls.

The war had been fought the last few years in the middle and southern states, but certainly the families in Killingworth prayed for the safe return of their friends, sons, and fathers. Records for the Continental Army list the names of twenty-five soldiers from Killingworth in the 7th Regiment of the Connecticut Division,[24] although there were no Davises on the list. The regiment fought

---

[24] Johnston, The Record of Connecticut Men in the Military & Naval Service During the War of the Revolution, 15.

at the Battles of Germantown, Pennsylvania, and Monmouth, New Jersey, and suffered through the winter at Valley Forge. On July 5, 1779, the Connecticut Division was camped near West Point guarding the Hudson River, when unexpectedly the war returned to New England.

A British fleet of more than forty ships was sighted at 5 a.m. on July 5, 1779, in the harbor of New Haven, 21 miles from Killingworth. By 8 a.m., 3,000 British troops led by Major General William Tryon had landed. Several hundred New Haven militiamen slowed the attack but were finally overwhelmed and had to give up the town. A company of Yale students, about seventy in number, commanded by George Welles of the Senior Class, assisted in checking the British advance.[25]

Messengers rode to the nearby towns including Killingworth for reinforcements on the morning of July 5. Since Connecticut laws required "every male citizen between the ages of sixteen and sixty shall serve in the state militia,"[26] it was certain that Daniel's father and uncles marched to New Haven with the Killingworth men in Colonel Worthington's Regiment of the 2nd Brigade. Could James Sr. possibly have been an officer in the militia? Maybe Daniel (later in life a Brigadier General in the New York Militia) inherited his ability to lead men from him.

The Killingworth troop arrived in New Haven with other militia that evening but were not strong enough to force the British regulars out of town. That night the invaders plundered the town, burning several buildings, but most of the town's hundreds of structures, including Yale College, were left intact.[27]

---

[25] Dexter, *Biographical Sketches of the Graduates of Yale College*, 89.
[26] Gerlander, "Understanding the Connecticut Militia During the Revolution".
[27] The commanding officer of a loyalist brigade fighting alongside the British, Colonel Edmund Fanning, a Yale graduate, influenced General Tryon to spare the city from destruction. Townshend, *The British Invasion of New Haven, Connecticut.*

Brigadier General Daniel Davis and the War of 1812

At daybreak the next morning, the Davises must have seen action when Colonel Worthington's regiment, along with militia from other Connecticut towns, battled the last British troops holding out on Beacon Hill. By the afternoon, all the invaders had retreated to their ships and sailed west.

George Washington ordered the Connecticut Division of the Continental Army to the coast; however, they did not arrive in time to stop the subsequent raids. The next few days the British fleet moved west along the coast, and their attack was more brutal than at New Haven. They burned the entire towns of Fairfield and Norwalk.

Although the Tryon raids achieved the British military goal to draw American forces away from West Point, the attacks backfired creating a surge in volunteers for the Continental Army, possibly thwarting the British plans to attack West Point.

Two years later in late October 1781, five year old Daniel might have assumed his older brother's chore of husking corn, as James Jr. fed the livestock, when his father arrived home with a copy of *The Gazette,* a newspaper published in New Haven. Perhaps it was their family custom that James Sr. read it to them. James Jr. would have washed his hands and left his boots outside, Hannah would be at her loom, and Daniel may have played with a "whirligig"[28] as James Davis, Sr., read aloud the heartening news that General Cornwallis had surrendered to George Washington at Yorktown, Virginia, marking the last major battle of the war.

---

[28] The whirligig was a simple whirling toy made from a circular disc (made of bone, clay, or even a spare button) with a string threaded through its center. By pulling the string tight and releasing it, children could set the whirligig whirring and buzzing. Pruitt, "13 Everyday Objects of Colonial America, History."

Daniel was seven years old, learning to read in 1783, when the Treaty of Paris was signed, formally ending the war. A century earlier in New England, the Puritans had established the tradition of ensuring their children could read so they could study the Bible. By 1783, as most New Englanders, the Davises likely continued the tradition. Reading secular literature was becoming common, such as Thomas Paine's *Common Sense*, Benjamin Franklin's Poor *Richard's Almanac*, and novels written by British authors. For example, *Robinson Crusoe* was very popular. Books could be purchased from traveling peddlers or mail ordered. At the end of the Revolution, among white New England males, more than 85 percent of the population was literate; the women's literacy rate was less than 50 percent.

Perhaps Daniel was taught to read with the same *New England Primer* that his older brother and his father had used. First published in 1688, an early edition may have helped his grandfather, Solomon Davis, learn how to read. The primer included illustrations and Puritan religious beliefs to teach reading skills. More than six million copies of the *New England Primer* were printed between 1681 and 1830.[29] In the spirit of the new nation, the Davises might also have bought a primer with "Americanized" words, which was published in 1783 by Noah Webster in nearby Hartford, Connecticut. *Webster's Speller* was entirely secular. It ended with two pages of important dates in American history, beginning with Columbus in 1492 and ending with the battle of Yorktown in 1781. There was no mention of God, the Bible, or sacred events.[30]

Daniel was ten years old in 1786. His education was likely seasonal, depending on the needs of the farm. During the summer he may have attended schooling along with his cousins

---

[29] Books That Shaped America.
[30] Noah Webster Reforms the Teaching of English in the United States.

and neighbors, perhaps taught by his father's aunt, Elizabeth Hull, at her house. During the rest of the year his home schooling would have resumed for a few hours each day after his work was done.

 Both James Jr. and Daniel would have routinely joined their father in the strenuous work, already familiar with principals of farming. Daniel's sister Lydia was six and likely could operate the spinning wheel as well as help her mother take care of her younger siblings, Asher, four, and Russell, two. Hannah had given birth to Daniel's fifth sibling, a boy named Norton. In the 18th century, the arrival of a newborn was viewed by the parents as a future beneficial laborer and an insurance policy for old age. The agrarian lifestyle common in America required large quantities of hard work, whether it was planting crops, feeding chickens, or mending fences. Most families simply could not afford the costs of raising a child from birth to adulthood without some compensating labor.[31]

 Although the September harvest was over the year of Norton's birth, Daniel and James Jr. were still busy taking care of the livestock. Daniel may have reminisced about his younger years when his major chores were hunting passenger pigeons, which supplemented their food, or killing rats in the "English"[32] barn to protect the corn stocks. A great deal of this maize was to feed a pair of oxen for plowing, a score of dairy cattle, about the same number of sheep, and a drove of pigs. Their three horses, for pulling their cart, grazed on grass in the summer and ate hay in the winter.

---

[31] Schuman, History of child labor in the United States.
[32] In some English barns two sets of doors on the opposite wall allowed wagons to be driven through the barn. The wagon drive floor also was used for threshing and winnowing; and the side bays had tie-ups for a few cattle and bin storage for grain. Overhead [were] bay lofts. Cunnigham, *Historic barns of Connecticut*, 5.

The days were shorter and after dark, perhaps their father began reading the newspaper aloud to the family. Also, he may have had James Jr. read to the family. One article they read could have been about Shay's Rebellion, which described how angry farmers in nearby Springfield, Massachusetts, took up arms, protesting high taxes imposed by the state of Massachusetts to pay the war debts, some losing their farms. The paper money issued by the Continental Congress from 1776 to 1779 was an unstable currency and had depreciated rapidly, adding to the economic dilemma.[33] If the older sons had been troubled by the events, James may have reassured them explaining that the Davises, as were most of the farmers in Connecticut, were well off during the war, selling livestock and food to the Continental army, producing saltpeter for the black powder mills,[34] and supplying the nearby shipyards with timber for their ships. The farmers were angry over the subsequent devaluation of the paper money, and had been paid only in part with silver coins. Then when the French entered the war, needing supplies, the farmers were paid entirely in gold or silver. In their prudence, the Davises had saved the coins during the revolution, which assured the

---

[33] By the end of 1778, Continentals retained from $\frac{1}{5}$ to $\frac{1}{7}$ of their face value. By 1780, the bills were worth $\frac{1}{40}$ of their face value. By May 1781, Continentals had become so worthless that they ceased to circulate as money. Benjamin Franklin noted that the depreciation of the currency had, in effect, acted as a tax to pay for the war. Wright, *One Nation Under Debt*, 49.

[34] Schenawolf, *Gunpowder and its Supply in the American Revolutionary War*. The Second Continental Congress even printed and distributed a pamphlet on how to make saltpeter and was willing to buy up all saltpeter produced at half a dollar per pound. The pamphlet recommended: "[that] vegetable and animal refuse containing nitrogen [were collected], the sweepings of slaughterhouses, weeds, etc., were collected into heaps in a shed or house where they were protected from the rain, and mixed with limestone, old mortar and ashes. The heaps were moistened from time to time with runnings from stables and other urine. When decomposition was complete, the heaps were leached with water, the liquor evaporated, and the saltpeter recrystallized."

boys that the family would get through the hard economic times after the war.

James Sr. may have had concerns himself. The forty acres he shared with his two brothers would not be enough to support their families when the next generation came of age.

Michael A. Ponzio

CHAPTER IV: Genesee Fever 1799

Daniel Davis's great-grandfather, Solomon Sr., may have descended from a Davis family originally from Boston. "According to family and local tradition, [they] came to Killingworth, Connecticut, from Long Island, the home of a large family of Davises who were evidently descendants of John [Davis] who came from Boston in 1655. A number of them settled in southern Connecticut: Guilford and Killingworth."[35]

The town of Killingworth was settled near the coast. As more land was needed, later generations moved inland. Solomon Sr. may have been granted 120 acres about five to ten miles from the coast, still part of Killingworth township. It was likely the parcel was completely forested, requiring hard work to clear enough land to support his family.[36]

Solomon Sr. likely passed his land to his three sons, each receiving 40 acres, a third of his land. Perhaps Solomon wrote a will similar to a testament recorded in 1728 by a farmer in

---

[35] Rootsweb, solomon-davis/individual.
[36] "Typical holdings averaged around 100 acres, 18. Plots were distributed in "rights," usually in twenty, forty or sixty-acre chunks, 13. Carly, Connecticut Historical and Architectural Resources Inventory 2013.

Fairfield, Connecticut, record: "I Ezekiel Sanford, of the town and county of Fairfield, in consideration of the natural love and affection I have for my sons Joseph, Lemuel and Samuel Sanford, (do give) as part of my estate, a parcel of land lying in ye peculiar between Fairfield and Danbury at Umpawaug Hill, so called . . . two hundred acre . . ."[37] The will continued to indicate how many acres he left his sons and the value of the land, about one English pound per acre.

In the next generation, Solomon Jr., Daniel's grandfather, may have also split his 40 acres into thirds and left Daniel's father, James Sr., about 13 acres, the rest to his two surviving brothers. They may have shared land, but it would have been difficult to support three large families on the combined 40 acres. To further complicate the situation, each year the soil had become more depleted. They may have been able to succeed on the less than nominal acreage by applying farming methods tested and advocated by George Washington. Such methods were rotating crops and fertilizing with manure and organic rich mud from creeks to increase productivity.

By 1776, throughout New England there was a shortage of enough farmland. New England's population had doubled since Daniel's grandfather's time. In the American colonies, 46% of children died by age five, but "New England's healthy climate (the cold winters killed the mosquitoes) and abundant food supply, resulted in the lowest death rate and highest birth rate of the colonies."[38]

When it was time for Daniel to be married and raise a family, his generation would likely have at least ten male inheritors in Killingworth, an average of only twelve acres for each. "The minimum for 'economic security' required at least twenty acres of cleared land, equally subdivided into three components: grain

---

[37] Colley, *"The Farms of Redding, Connecticut and Colonial Farming Page"*.
[38] "The Growth of the Colonies"

tillage, hay fields, and pastures."³⁹ Perhaps some of the Davises could have taken up skilled trades instead of farming, but in a small community such as Killingworth there would be few opportunities for the required apprenticeship. The problem is summarized well in a historical document of 18th century Connecticut agriculture, "Our lands are cleared and settled; our farms in general will not bear a further division; unless there be some new resource our most active, our industrious and enterprising young men will emigrate to those parts of the continent where there is more vacant territory."⁴⁰

The need for more land was enough motivation for the Davises to relocate. It would not be easy, the long journey, the hard work cultivating the raw frontier, but the price of land in western New York was much lower, selling for $1.20 to $3.50 per acre compared to $10 to 20 an acre in Connecticut.⁴¹ And living in Killingworth where people were loyal Congregationalists, it is questionable whether the Davises had been affected by the evangelistic Great Awakening. The religious movement, however, had influenced people to worship in a new way and many emigrated to escape the conformity of the Congregationalists.

Where was new land to settle? Before the American Revolution, the native Iroquois had formed a powerful confederacy, preventing settlement west of the Hudson and Mohawk Valleys. The six Iroquois nations of the confederacy split during the Revolution, the majority fighting for the British against the Americans. In 1778, George Washington ordered

---

³⁹ Volo, Quora, How many acres could a family farm manage in the 18th century thirteen colonies?
⁴⁰ Olson, *"Agricultural Economy and the Population in Eighteenth-Century Connecticut",* 18.
⁴¹ Siles, *A vision of wealth: speculators and settlers in the Genesee Country of New York 1788 1800,* 87.

General Sullivan to conduct a "scorched-earth" strategy against the hostile tribes. By the following year, Sullivan's forces had burned over forty Iroquois villages along with their corn fields and winter food stocks. To the Iroquois, President Washington was afterwards known as "Town Destroyer." A few bands of the Iroquois survivors were scattered across western New York, but the majority had fled to Canada. Many perished due to lack of food and shelter.

The defeated Iroquois had forfeited rights to their territory; however, in the treaty ending the conflict, the "Iroquois were grateful to Washington. It was he who had shown them mercy and provided for them at least a portion of their ancient domain in New York, when the entire country clamored for their removal into the west."[42] The United States still upheld the rights of the native Americans to their lands in western New York, three million acres west of the Genesee River.

Nevertheless, Massachusetts required compensation to give up their 17th century claim to western New York. The initial land company making these payments defaulted, so they sold most of the land to Robert Morris, "financier of the American Revolution,"[43] who purchased the land, then sold it to a group of Dutch bankers, who formed a business named the Holland Land Company. Other tracts of land were sold to Herman LeRoy, a banker in New York City; Sir William Pulteney, an English businessman; and others, but the "purchased lands"

---

[42] Parker, *"The Senecas in the War of 1812."*
[43] When the Revolutionary war broke out in 1775, Robert Morris used his shipping connections and financial acumen to help amass the money and supplies to create an American army and navy. As superintendent of finance, he hounded the states throughout the war for funds to keep soldiers armed and fed. He often used his personal credit to secure loans for the colonial forces, and many ships in his mercantile fleet became "privateers," attacking British ships and seizing their cargo. Without Robert Morris, the American colonies' attempt to throw off British rule could never have succeeded. Silsby, *"The Holland Land Company in Western New York".*

could not legally be sold to settlers until they persuaded the Iroquois to cede the land. In 1797, Robert Morris's son, Thomas; representatives from the Holland Land Company; and the U.S. government held a council at Big Tree (Geneseo, New York) attended by the Iroquois leaders who included male sachems and the principal women. The Iroquois women raised the crops, "owned the land," and played a significant role in tribal governance. Chief Red Jacket, a prominent chief, withdrew with anger, but giving way to "a custom that when land sales were considered, if the warriors and women were dissatisfied with the course of the sachems, they had a right to take the subject out of their hands."[44] Mary Jemison[45], of the Seneca tribe, was instrumental in securing several reservations encompassing a total of 200,000 acres, as well as annual annuities. However, "it was necessary to give presents to influential women of the tribe and to make generous bribes to several chiefs in order to persuade the Indians to grant their land rights to the Holland Land Company."[46]

By 1800, 60,000 immigrants, many from Killingworth, were affected by "Genesee Fever," emigrating from New England to settle in western New York. Most settlers headed west of the Genesee River, beyond the "Military Tract," a great swath of two million acres between Utica and Canandaigua that had been set aside to award to veterans of the Continental Army who had fought in the American Revolution.

Some immigrants traveled during the winter transporting their belongings and families in sleighs, following the roads to

---

[44] McIntosh, History of Wayne County, New York 1789-1877.

[45] Abducted at the age of fifteen by Shawnee Indians and French soldiers, Mary Jemison was adopted by the Seneca tribe. She married a Seneca man in 1765 and gave birth to eight children. She lived the rest of her life among Indians and published her story in 1824 at the age of eighty-one. *Lapham's Quarterly*.

[46] Silsby, "The Holland Land Company in Western New York"

the west. Those with better means hired sloops to transport their furniture up the Hudson River to Albany. They used wagons to continue to their destination or transferred to bateaux, which rivermen poled up the Mohawk River, portaged to Lake Ontario, and continued by water to western New York.

Like the majority of immigrants, it is likely the Davises went "turnpiking,"[47] traveling overland, carrying their basic household possessions like cooking pots, tools, and clothes by wagon or ox cart. Most likely Daniel Davis's family would have goaded their oxen to pull their carts along the Boston Post Road to Hartford, taken the Greenwood Road through Pittsfield, then followed the Rensselaer Pike to Albany. Then they would have followed the Mohawk Pike to Utica and traversed the final 160 miles on the Great Genesee Pike to Ganson's Settlement, the name of the cluster of cabins which eventually grew into the village of LeRoy, New York.

---

[47] Ellis, "The Yankee Invasion of New York, 1783-1850," 5.

ns and the War of 1812

Michael A. Ponzio

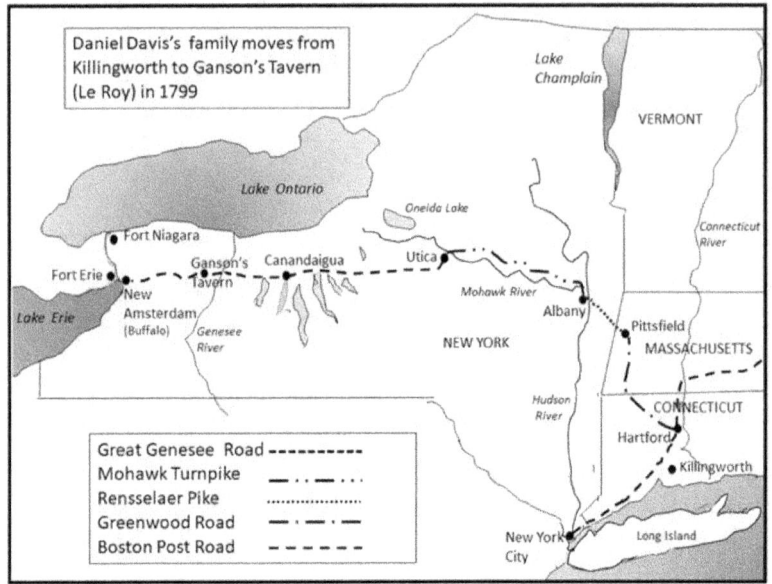

CHAPTER V: Move to New York 1800

When did Daniel Davis arrive in LeRoy, New York, originally known as Ganson's settlement? Beers Gazetteer and Biographical Record of Genesee County lists three separate dates. On page 460 of Beers, the record states: "Daniel Davis was among the earliest of the pioneers. He, soon after his arrival, married Naomi Le Barron, who had emigrated to the [Ganson's] settlement with the family of Philemon Nettleton from Killingworth, Connecticut in 1797."[48]

On page 461, also from Beers, is a list "of the early settlers of LeRoy," which included, "General Daniel Davis arriving in 1799."[49] And a third date is listed in Beers: "James [Daniel's older brother] and Johanah (Wilcox) Davis, came from Killingworth, Connecticut, with an ox-team, and first settled about three miles east of Ganson's, on a farm taken up by Gen. Daniel Davis about 1800."[50]

---

[48] Beers, Gazetteer and Biographical Source No. 1: Record of Genesee County, N.Y. 1788-1890, 460.
[49] Ibid, 461.
[50] Ibid, 524.

Another source cites a later date, "General Daniel Davis, who located in town in 1801, was also an early tavern keeper."[51]

An 1858 interview of a resident of LeRoy recorded that Daniel Davis was in Ganson's settlement in 1799 with his future brother-in-law, preparing the homestead before they brought their relatives from Killingworth. John Samson's History of Brigadier Daniel Davis included an extract from the LeRoy Gazette in 1858: "In the same year (1799) Daniel Davis and Philemon Nettleton commenced improvements and having built a log house, returned to Killingworth, Connecticut for their friends. Mr. Nettleton brought his family and Mr. Davis that of his father. In the family of Mr. Nettleton was Miss Naomi Le Barron, a sister of Mrs. Nettleton."[52]

The LeRoy Gazette also stated, "Charles Wilbur having been appointed a Justice of the Peace, probably performed the first marriage ceremony in Ganson's settlement in the autumn of 1800, when Daniel Davis and Naomi Le Barron, Gardner Carver and Lydia Davis [Daniel's sister] were respectively united in matrimony."[53]

In conclusion, Daniel initially arrived in 1799, prepared the farmstead in western New York, returning with the family before the date of his marriage in the autumn of 1800. Another event narrows down the period of his arrival. Genealogy records list the birthdate of Daniel's nephew, Lewis, as April 9, 1800, and the birthplace as LeRoy. Lewis was the first child of James Jr. [Daniel's older brother] and his wife, Jehannah Wilcox.[54]

---

[51] Gray, LeRoy Town, Genesee County, New York Genweb Project.
[52] Samson, History of Brigadier Daniel Davis, Extracts from Peep at the Pioneers by Clorindia Buell, LeRoy Gazette, June 9, 1856, 10.
[53] Ibid, 10.
[54] Davis, "Genealogical records of James M. Davis Family by Betty Neracker Davis."

Their new home was at a place called Limerock, two miles east of Ganson's Tavern on the Great Genesee Road, (East Main Street in present day LeRoy).

What members of the family moved to western New York with Daniel Davis? The earlier citation stated after scouting out land on the frontier, Daniel had returned to Killingworth and 'brought back his family' to western New York, so his father, James Sr., 52, and his mother, Hannah, must have been with him. The recollection of a neighbor about 1807 placed his parents at the homestead a few miles from Ganson's settlement. "At Limerock we find old Mr. James Davis and wife, an aged couple from Connecticut. They lived in a log hut on the north side of the road. Their descendants were James, Daniel, Norton, Calvin, and a daughter [Lydia]."[55]

Daniel, now twenty-three, certainly showed maturity and incentive by traveling hundreds of miles to western New York to get the farm ready, returning to guide the family west. Perhaps his father relinquished some of the leadership to his son for the journey. Did the abilities as a leader emerge in Daniel's early years which later led to his promotion as a general in the militia?

His older brother James Jr. and his wife moved to New York with him. "In 1799 . . . among these early settlers was James Davis, Jr., [who] came into the [Ganson] settlement."[56] Daniel's future wife, Naomi Le Barron, certainly his fiancé before the move, accompanied the Nettleton family along with the Davises to western New York.

Daniel's sister Lydia and brothers Calvin and Norton must have been in the traveling party, but the fate of his other brothers, Asher and Russell, is unknown.[57]

---

[55] Samson, History of Brigadier Daniel Davis, Extracts from Recollections of Simon Pierson, LeRoy Gazette, March 26, 1856., 11.
[56] Beers, Gazetteer and Biographical Source, 461.
[57] Samson, *History of Brigadier Daniel Davis.*

The Davises and Nettletons moving together, probably a group of at least fourteen adults and two Nettleton infants, might have traveled in a small convoy of wagons and oxcarts. The adults would have alternated between walking and riding. Those guiding the oxen would have walked to the left of the team, driving the oxen using voice commands. Goad sticks were rarely needed for the best trained animals, the ideal oxen being gentle, patient, and reliable.[58] The parents may have ridden more frequently, the Nettleton toddler and baby riding with their mother. They also likely had a few horses. The oxen rendered a slow procession, but they would need the sturdy animals to plow when they arrived at their new home. "At an ox pace of two miles per hour, including rest breaks, the average rate of travel across a ten-hour day was about one and one-half miles per hour,"[59] or fifteen miles per day. It probably took them almost a month to complete the trip.

Perhaps they moved in late August 1799 to avoid the snow and cold weather and the muddy roads of early spring. The Boston Post Road to Hartford, a well-maintained road of crushed gravel, would have allowed the party to make it past Hartford the first day, camping in a meadow, perhaps after asking permission from the landowner before they pitched their tents. If they had continued early the next day, taking the Greenwood Road, by the early afternoon they would arrive in Pittsfield. At the outskirts of town, they may have joined an encampment of other travelers.

In 1799 a movement similar to the "Great Awakening" that occurred fifty years earlier was sweeping across New York. This

---

[58] Emigrants wanted their wagons safely drawn by strong oxen, horned steers at least four years old, of calm and gentle temperament, accustomed to sudden movements and loud noises, and trained from birth to obey verbal and visual cues. Ford and Kreutzer, *"Oxen: Engines of Overland Emigration"*.
[59] Ford and Kreutzer, "Oxen: Engines of Overland Emigration".

"Second Great Awakening"[60] was the beginning of a series of revivals which would spread across the United States over the next decades. Possibly the Nettletons and the Davises, accustomed to attending Calvinistic homilies their whole lives, witnessed a sermon by one of the circuit preachers during their journey. And what an experience had the preacher been "Crazy Dow."[61] Several congregations had rejected Lorenzo Dow, a poorly educated Methodist preacher, for his unusual deliveries, compelling him to become an itinerant circuit preacher, railing against Universalism, atheism, deism, Calvinism, and especially the Catholic Jesuits. He was in Pittsfield in 1799. If Daniel didn't experience one of Dow's sermons during their trip, he was sure to have crossed paths with one of the evangelistic preachers because they followed the pioneers to western New York and typically held the sermons outdoors.

The Nettleton-Davis party would have traveled from Pittsfield for a few days on the Rensselaer Pike arriving north of Albany, where they crossed the Hudson River on the Hamilton-Scotts Ferry.[62] The next two days were easy going on the Mohawk Turnpike following the north side of the river to Utica,

---

[60] Second Great Awakening was a Protestant religious revival in the United States from 1795 to 1835. Meetings were held in small towns and large cities throughout the country, and the unique frontier institution known as the camp meeting began. Many churches experienced a great increase in membership, particularly among Methodist and Baptist churches. Petruzzello, *"Second Great Awakening"*.

[61] Dow's public speaking mannerisms were like nothing ever seen before among the typically conservative churchgoers of the time. He shouted, he screamed, he cried, he begged, he flattered, he insulted, and he challenged people and their beliefs. He told stories and made jokes. *"Who Was Lorenzo Dow?"*

[62] This boat ferry was used principally during the turnpike and stagecoach days. It was used until the building of the Union Bridge in 1804 near the "Waterford & Stage House", classed a boat and ice-ferry and connected Waterford and Lansingburg [Troy]. Hammersley, *The History of Waterford, New York.*

a busy new town, where they crossed "a bridge built in 1797, at the foot of Genesee Street."[63]

From Utica they would take the Great Genesee Road for 150 miles to LeRoy. West of Utica they passed through a small Iroquois reservation of the Onondaga Nation, most of the New Englanders seeing Native Americans for the first time. The party traversed the Military Tract, a fertile area where many veterans of the Revolution had settled, developing thriving towns. Within a week, they reached Hartford, present day Avon, on the east bank of the Genesee River. They crossed the river by way of a rope ferry operated by the owner of Berry's Tavern. The first bridge across the river was not constructed until 1804. After camping on the west side of the river, the next day they traveled through the wilderness, the land thick with forests of oak and chestnut trees. Just east of Big Springs, present day Caledonia, they might have noticed Seneca natives from their nearby village of Canawaugus. Ten more miles and they arrived at their homestead on the north side of the Great Genesee Road at a place called Limerock, three miles east of Allen's Creek (Oatka Creek) about a mile east of Ganson's Tavern.

The Great Genesee Road, which approximates the present New York State Road 5, had been laid out in 1794 between Utica and Avon, following the well beaten trails used by the Iroquois for centuries traveling between the Hudson River and Lake Erie.[64] On early maps of LeRoy, the pike was called the Niagara Road and east of Ganson's Tavern, the State Road. In 1798, the road was extended through LeRoy to Buffalo, and the road west of Ganson's was locally called Buffalo Road. If the Davises had

---

[63] Greene, *History of the Mohawk Valley: Gateway to the West 1614-1925*. 1223.

[64] "The trails of the Senecas were the chosen routes for public roads in later days, evincing undoubted taste in civil engineering." Beers, *Gazetteer and Biographical Source*, 12.

arrived in early April 1800, they may have been subject to tolls. On April 1, 1800, the Seneca Road Company took over maintenance of the Great Genesee Road, charging tolls of eight cents per mile for a cart and two oxen, twelve cents per mile for a wagon and two horses, and the same if they pulled a sleigh between December 15 and March 15.[65]

---

[65] In 1798 the enlarged former Indian path extended from the Seneca village at Canawaugus (now part of present-day Caledonia) west to New Amsterdam (now Buffalo) and on to Lewiston on the Niagara River. Also known as the Niagara Rd the Genesee Rd and the Buffalo Rd or simply the State Road, it was renamed the Seneca Turnpike during the 19th century. It quickly became the most important east-west highway for white settlers as well as the principal land route for shipments of salt, wheat, and other products to the eastern markets. Smith, *"A History of the Early Development of the Towns of LeRoy, Bergen, Sweden, Clarkson and Hamlin New York"*, 59.

Michael A. Ponzio

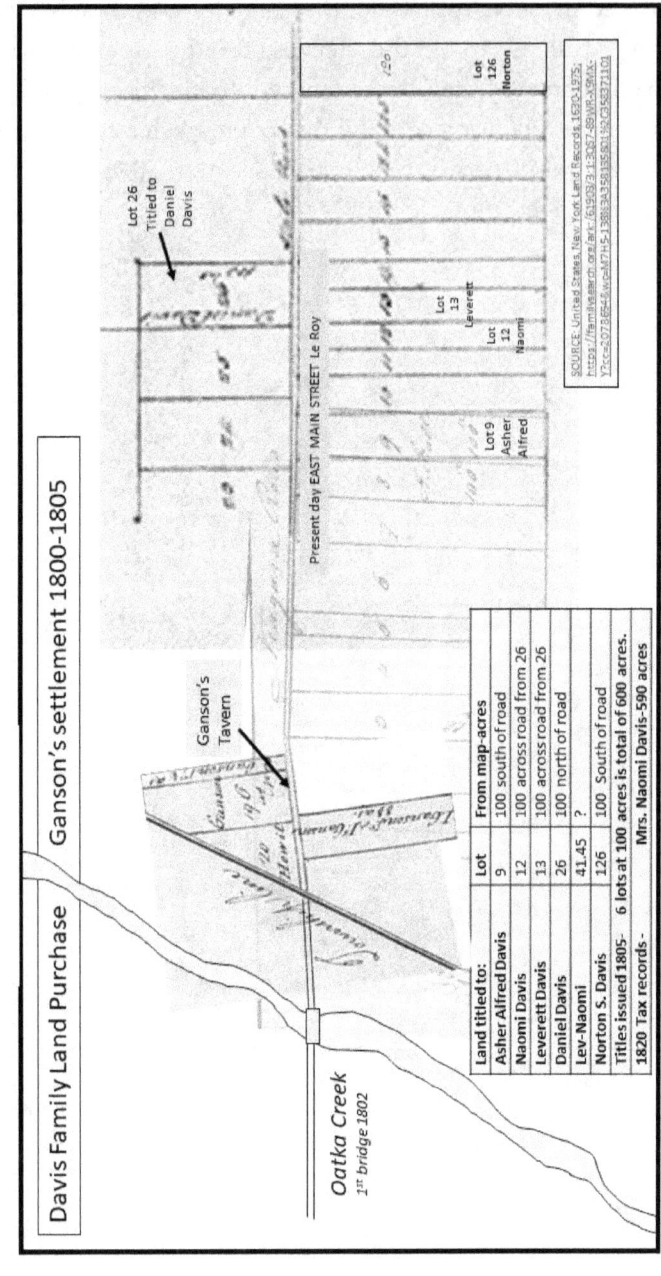

Brigadier General Daniel Davis and the War of 1812

Michael A. Ponzio

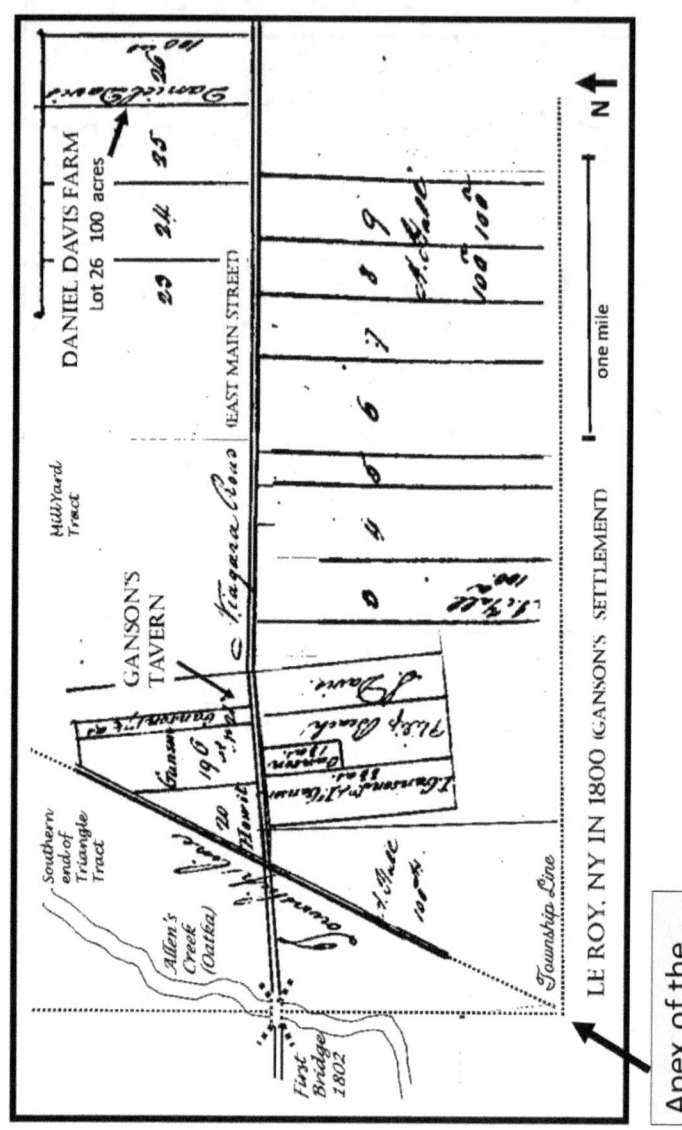

CHAPTER VI: 1800-1804 Ganson's Settlement

By April 1800, the Davises and Nettletons had arrived a few miles east of Ganson's settlement, their cabins ready for occupancy at Lot 26 of Township No.1, a 100-acre tract that Daniel Davis had purchased.[66] The deed to the land, transferred to Daniel in 1805, indicates he paid 300 dollars.[67] Three years earlier at the council of Big Tree, the Holland Land Company had paid the Seneca nation "less than a third of a cent an acre."[68]

Perhaps he had purchased the land with a down payment, receiving the deed after he paid in full. The United States, New York Land Records, 1630-1975, Genesee County database also lists that Daniel purchased five other lots, averaging about 100 acres each and received the deeds in 1805. Two lots were directly

---

[66] "United States, New York Land Records, 1630-1975", Index of Deeds, Genesee County, 258.
[67] When the first settlers arrived in 1789 at Canandaigua, NY, east of Ganson's, farm lots, averaging 100 acres, were priced at $0.56 an acre. Canandaigua had only 99 people, but by 1800, it numbered nearly 1,153 and farmland prices had increased to an average of $3.00 an acre, the price that Daniel Davis had paid. Siles, *"A Vision of Wealth: Speculators and Settlers in the Genesee Country of New York 1798-1800."*, 87, 151.
[68] LaChiusa, "History of Buffalo, 1800."

across the Niagara Road (present day East Main Street, LeRoy, New York). The purchase of these six lots, totaling approximately 600 acres, agrees with the 1820 tax records which show Naomi Davis owned 590 acres.[69]

Why weren't at least some of the deeds issued to James Sr., Daniel's father, or James Jr., his older brother? Also puzzling, why are most of the deeds issued in his children's names? (Some were not even born by 1805). Was he looking to the future and breaking the tradition of holding the land to keep siblings and children on the land to work the farm in his old age? Thus, they would grow up already owning their future inheritance. Perhaps Daniel had a brilliant idea. He had bought the lots on individual contracts, so if he could not keep payments up on all of the lots, he could at least retain one or two.

Deed issued 1805	Lot	Birth Year
Leverett/Asher/Alfred	9	1809/1803/1801
Naomi	12	Daniel's wife
Leverett	13	1809
Daniel	26	Himself
Leverett-Naomi	41	1809/Daniel's wife
Norton S.	126	1786 Daniel's younger brother
Titles issued 1805-		6 lots at 100 acres totals 600 acres.
1820 Tax records -		Mrs. Naomi Davis owns 590 acres.

The Davis family was more fortunate than many of the settlers. The land companies were lenient and down payments were rare; however, many settlers' efforts were unsuccessful and they failed to make the annual payments, losing their land. "Few

---

[69] Samson, *History of Brig. Gen. Daniel Davis*.

of the settlers could meet the prompt payment demanded. Most of them were obliged to submit to the terms of renewed contracts. Un-toward years followed, and the finale was the loss, with many of their improvements, while many were obliged to sell at a sacrifice, and renew in some western region."[70]

Some of the early land agents permitted them to pay with farm produce or with their labor. Some purchasers who desired to make an immediate settlement and had farms in the east but little capital were allowed to trade their farms for equivalent land on their purchases.[71]

The contracts to buy land usually required from four to six equal, annual payments. Where would Daniel get the cash to pay when most of the local economy involved bartering? Likely, the down payment he brought with him from Connecticut. One possible source which brought in a few dollars for the settlers was to sell wood ash. They burned trees and stumps cleared for cultivation and collected the piles of ash along with their fireplace cleanout. A teamster hauled the ash to Lake Ontario, and it was shipped to Montreal to make potash. Wolves' hides may have brought in a couple of dollars. There were few genuine inns to accommodate travelers along the frontier road, and there were many immigrants needing overnight shelter. Almost every cabin along the turnpike was a "tavern" or "inn," serving food and strong cider, as well as renting beds, frequently shared by strangers. In fact, "Daniel Davis was a tavern-keeper east of the village."[72]

O. Turner, the author of the 1851 publication *History of the Pioneer Settlement of Phelps and Gorman's Purchase and Morris Reserve*, sums up the way most settlers purchased land on the frontier of western New York. "Both the English and the Dutch companies

---

[70] Turner, 541.
[71] Siles, *A vision of wealth: speculators and settlers in the Genesee Country*. 95.
[72] Beers, Gazetteer and Biographical Source, 481.

were satisfied with reasonable returns and patient under the delays of payment. If any wrong policy was pursued it was a fixing of too high prices upon land but in many instances, almost interminable credits were given; and that enabled men to possess, and finally pay for land, who could not have done so, if [down] payment [even] at a very low rate had been demanded in hand. There is not in the history of the world a better example of the advantages of credit than is furnished in the settlement of all this region."[73]

The Davises had to clear land for spring planting. "A family with sufficient sons could clear about four acres of woodland a year. A single farmer walking behind a plow could turn about two acres a day."[74] The Davis family had five men available to work: James Sr., 52; James Jr., 25; Daniel 23; Calvin, 19; and Norton, 13. Three more men from the Nettleton family were available: Abel Sr., 55; Abel Jr., 25, and Philemon, 23. Eight men with axes and a few teams of oxen likely would have been able to clear enough land to grow crops to feed two families, with supplemental supplies and meat procured by hunting in the extensive forests. The country abounded in game. "The deer were at their very door."[75] Perhaps a few young men, the sons of the twenty-one farmsteads[76] near Ganson's tavern, may have helped, trading their labor for future payback or other means of bartering.

---

[73] Turner, *History of the Pioneer Settlement*, 250.
[74] Volo, Quora, How many acres could a family farm manage in the 18th century thirteen colonies?
[75] Beers, 466.
[76] John Maule, an English gentleman, passed through on the way to see Niagara Falls on August 20, 1800, accompanied by Hotbread, chief of the nearby Seneca village of Canawaugus. Maule wrote in his diary: "Ganson's [Tavern] is now in the midst of a flourishing township, in which 21 families are already settled." Beers, *Gazetteer and Biographical Source*, 17.

Working during all daylight hours, from the "time they can see to the time they can't see," the Davises certainly rested on the Sabbath. With no organized church west of the Genesee River, but inheriting the customs from their Congregational upbringing, perhaps the Davises took turns reading aloud passages from the Bible to each other on Sunday. All the adults were literate. If they assembled with others for worship, it might have been in a neighbor's barn or in a settler's cabin. In 1801, some groups worshiped at the first schoolhouse, a primitive log structure. The *Second Great Awakening*, which began in 1795, had spread to the frontier by 1800. It's possible the Davises were in attendance when an itinerant preacher arrived to conduct a sermon, perhaps at Ganson's Tavern. Records show the first sermon at the site of present day LeRoy was delivered by Reverend David Perry, a Presbyterian missionary from the Berkshire and Columbia Missionary Society of Massachusetts. He would be the first of many more that would visit over the next decades. Ganson's Tavern also lodged travelers, and it's likely the "saddlebag" preacher's bed and board were bartered for his sermon. So common were the visits of the Methodist circuit riders that "The homes which circuit riders lodged came to be known as Methodist Taverns."[77] And according to another traveler who stopped at Ganson's, the traveling preachers' sermons were very much needed.[78]

Although the majority of the traveling preachers visiting the frontier towns in western New York were Methodist circuit

---

[77] Wigger, John H., Taking Heaven by Storm, 72.
[78] Timothy Bigalow travels: "Ganson's is a miserable log house. We hastened our departure, because the landlord was drunk and the miserable log cabin house was crowded with a dozen workmen reeking with rain and sweat and we were annoyed with plaintive and frightful cries and screams of a crazy woman in the next room." Belluscio, *"Ganson's Tavern"*.

riders,[79] the Ganson's settlement's most frequent missionaries were Presbyterian.[80]

When Reverend Perry gave his sermon at Ganson's settlement in 1800, in attendance was a man named Carver, who had been a member of the Congregational church (as had been the Davises) before he moved to the frontier. Perhaps Reverend Perry sensed the man's strong faith. Before he departed, he encouraged Mr. Carver to hold services on the Sabbath. In 1802, a second Presbyterian traveling preacher arrived in Ganson's settlement, Reverend James Hotchkin; he found that Mr. Carver had abandoned his services after a season, in consequence of the neglect of attendance.[81]

A missionary from the Episcopal Church performed services in 1802 and returned in 1804 to give a sermon at the schoolhouse located in present day Trigon Park. Perhaps the Davises attended a variety of sermons, Methodist, Presbyterian, and Episcopal, depending on what circuit riding preacher was in town. The Congregationalists did not tend to send out missionaries. It is possible the Davises worshiped with immigrants from Scotland, who had settled Big Springs only three miles away. In 1802, the Scots "gathered at the house of Peter Campbell to establish the Caledonia Presbyterian Religious Society."[82] In 1805, they were officially organized as the First Presbyterian Church of

---

[79] Methodists were among the fastest growing churches in America, between 1770 and 1820. Methodists achieved a virtual miracle of growth, rising from fewer than 1,000 members to more than 250,000, becoming almost ten times the size of the Congregationalists, America's largest denomination in 1776. Key to the Methodist success was a dedicated contingent of itinerant preachers, or circuit riders. Wigger, *"Holy Knock'em Down Preachers"*.
[80] Beers, 490.
[81] Hotchkin, A History of the Purchase and Settlement of Western New York, 90, 548.
[82] Caledonia First Presbyterian Church.

Caledonia, meeting for years at Campbell's house for Sunday worship, until they built a small stone church in 1827."[83]

Daniel and his family most likely became Presbyterian due to the exposure to these missionaries and the nearby church in Big Springs. Four generations of his Davis descendants were Presbyterian.

Franklin Davis, great-great-great-grandnephew of Daniel Davis and resident of LeRoy, stated his father and grandfather were Presbyterians, as well as himself. Mary Ann Bovee Davis, the wife of Lewis Davis, Daniel Davis's nephew, was Presbyterian.[84]

In 1800, the state assessed taxes for the first time on the settlers west of the Genesee River. There were 142 individuals named on the tax rolls. The taxes based on the 1800 census listed 728 males, 340 females, 7 free blacks, and 9 slaves, for a total of 1,084 settlers in western New York[85] from Canandaigua to New Amsterdam (Buffalo).[86] Daniel Davis was listed on the roll as the owner of 572 acres and paid $0.72 in taxes.[87]

Several years before 1800, Northampton was the first "official" name given to the designated township by the state of New York, which included Ganson's settlement and Big Springs. Town meetings were held in the village of Big Springs, three miles east of the Davis farm. One of the officers chosen was John Ganson Sr., owner of the tavern. A subject of discussion was to "remind the farmers a bounty of $1 per hide was offered,

---

[83] Ibid.
[84] Davis, Mary Ann, Obituary.
[85] Beers, *Gazetteer and Biographical Source*, 457.
[86] The early village of Buffalo is briefly known as "New Amsterdam." But early residents do not approve of the name. They intend to call their new home "Buffalo." Although no one seems to know exactly where the name came from, it sticks. The name may have been adopted from a local Indian word, "Buffaloe." Or perhaps it came from "beau fleuve," French for beautiful river. LaChiusa, *"History of Buffalo, 1800"*.
[87] North, *"Our County and Its People"*, 74.

such was the havoc of the wolves among the herds."[88] One hundred dollars was raised "for destroying wolves and paying other contingent charges of the town." It was voted that the "wolfs head must have the entire skin thereon."[89]

It is highly likely that Daniel Davis was present at the Northampton town meeting held in Big Springs in 1801 because the officers voted for him to assume the responsibility of pathmaster.[90] Each road district had a "pathmaster" who supervised road maintenance and had the power to annually assess each male resident several days of labor on the road. Clearing the woodlands and maintaining the dirt roads, especially after the damages of storms, was crucial.[91]

Had the people chosen Daniel for this position because he had shown the ability to lead during his short time in the community? The majority of the settlers in western New York were from New England, and most of those were "Connecticut Yankees" known for their individualistic, self-sufficient, and independent character. Ellis describes the Yankee invasion of New York: "Settlers are continually pouring in from the Connecticut hive, which throws off its annual swarms of intelligent, industrious, and enterprising settlers, the best qualified of any men in the world to subdue and civilize the wilderness."[92] What methods did Daniel use to influence the settlers to contribute "several days of labor on the road"? Did he lead by example, diving into hard work himself? Perhaps he convinced them of the worth of a common goal.

Did Daniel Davis muster the needed labor to maintain and develop the roads with the goal of keeping pace with the local

---

[88] Ibid., 466.
[89] Turner, History of the Pioneer Settlement of Phelps and Gorman's Purchase and Morris Reserve, 416.
[90] Beers, 417.
[91] Barber, Jedediah, "Homer Grows Rapidly in the 1800s".
[92] Ellis, "The Yankee Invasion of New York, 1783-1850, 8.

economy? Many new settlers' cabins, a land office, the first schoolhouse, a grist mill, and a larger tavern-inn were built in the first few years after the Davises' arrival. "Upon the opening of new roads, and the completion of the surveys of the Holland Land Company in 1802, the whole section became alive with immigrants. The Ganson tavern was required to be enlarged, so the log tavern was razed to the ground, and a frame building erected in its place as a necessity from the increased travel."[93] The "modern" tavern and large inn was a significant improvement over the old log cabin. The new structure included a ballroom, where bachelors and single women gathered at "paring bees" for dancing to a local fiddler who provided the music. Perhaps Daniel's eighteen-year-old brother, Norton S., attended.

During the year Daniel served as pathmaster, several important roads were cut through the thick forest. A road was built from Batavia to the three mills the Bush family had erected on Tonawanda Creek. Also in 1801, the first road from Ganson's settlement to Lake Ontario was blazed, which later would be Lake Street in the future village of LeRoy. As Beers wrote: "The first road was opened in 1801, when the Lake Road was surveyed and opened four rods wide from LeRoy to the lake."[94] The road passed through the future site of the village of Bergen, stimulating the community's growth, and was vital for trade coming via Lake Ontario. In 1821, when the Erie Canal opened, it intersected the road, linking LeRoy to the vital water routes to Lake Erie, Albany, and New York City via the Hudson River.

Daniel was again called in 1801 to assume a leadership role. When he lived in Killingworth, he was likely in the militia, enlisting when he was sixteen. During his role in the Connecticut

---

[93] Beers, Gazetteer and Biographical Source, 455.

[94] Ibid., 326.

militia, perhaps he acquired a quality that impressed his peers in New York because on the first day of militia training at the Ganson farm, Daniel was chosen as lieutenant, reporting to the company officer, Captain Joseph Hewitt. John Ganson's son, James, was selected as ensign. The small troop of citizen soldiers included twenty-one militiamen.

"One day in each year, between September 1st and October 15th, at a place designated by the brigade officer, the regiment was directed to assemble for a general training."[95] For the next several years, the militia conducted most of the training sessions either at the Ganson farm or the Davis farm.

The training days were festive occasions. The people from the surrounding area were entertained by the action, and food and drink were provided. [The training session] "usually closed with a sham fight and often with a real one, particularly among the Indians, who were always out in 'full feather' to imbibe the 'fire water' and enjoy the sights."[96]

Perhaps, with the upbringing from a practical and efficient Yankee family, Daniel scheduled the militia training day in the following year to coincide with a need for manpower, using the militiamen, when "the first bridge over the Oatka was built in 1802. It was a memorable event. James Ganson was the contractor, and Charles Wilbur and Jotham Curtis the commissioners. Two hundred dollars in addition to $50 voted by the town had been raised for its construction. Laborers and a derrick, etc., had been obtained from Canandaigua, and a general 'bee' raised for the work of laying the timbers over the stream, made of split chestnut logs. A shanty for the men, and for providing entertainment for the occasion, was erected on the bank of the Oatka, and the work was commenced and finished in five days. Mrs. John Ganson, in her old age, informed the

---

[95] Ibid., 200.
[96] Beers, Gazetteer and Biographical Source, 456.

writer that she was the hostess that made provision for the entertainment, which was abundant in substantials, and not wanting in doughnuts and gingerbread, and of the liquids 'old rye' was not without a fair representation."[97]

The bridge built in 1802 was the first of four LeRoy Main Street bridges. The 1802 bridge was built of wood; 1823 of stone; 1855 of iron; and 1908 of concrete.[98]

Hopefully, with Daniel's civic duties he still had time to continue clearing and cultivating his land. The Davises likely grew corn, which they could take to three nearby mills. They may have taken their corn to John Ganson's primitive mill until 1803, when two partners, Stoddard and Piatt, started operation of a mill at Buttermilk Falls[99] about three miles to the west of the Davis farm on Allen's Creek (Oatka). The Davises could take their corn to another grist mill the same distance east at Big Springs, operated by John McKay.[100]

The Davises and Nettletons had moved together to western New York, intermarried, and may have lived on the same land the first year after their arrival. Richard M. Stoddard, in 1802, opened the first land office. He was the local agent of the "Triangle Tract," erecting the first building on the west side of the Oatka, a land office built of logs at the eventual location of the corner of Main and Mill streets.[101] Perhaps the Nettletons helped Daniel clear and plow his land and the Davises returned the favor at Philemon's farm. Records show that he bought a

---

[97] Ibid., 455.
[98] Leroy, New York Historical Marker.
[99] Beers described the "old" Buttermilk Falls:, "the stream was clear, full, and flowing over a rapid of 60 feet in extent and a fall of 11 feet. The name [Buttermilk] was attached to the falls from the earliest period, but of which it has since been ruthlessly robbed and applied to the "big fall" two miles below." [the present-day Buttermilk Falls]. *Gazetteer and Biographical Source*, 452.
[100] Ibid., 451.
[101] Ibid., 458.

tract a few miles north of present day LeRoy near Fort Hill likely, on credit, as records show he received his deed in 1804.

By 1803, the Davises had been at their new home for three years, during which time immigrants had been pouring into western New York. The increase in population had compelled the state to create Genesee County, partitioned from the larger tract of Ontario County. At the same time, the township of Northampton was divided into north and south, with Ganson's settlement included in the new township of Southampton. Joseph Ellicott, the leader of the original surveying party for the Holland Land Purchase, built a courthouse ten miles northwest of Ganson's settlement, founding the village of Batavia, which became the county seat.[102] Ellicott named the village after the Batavian Republic, the homeland of his employers, the Dutch owners of the Holland Land Company.

In April 1803, Daniel Davis, perhaps recognized for two years serving as second officer of his militia company, was elected as captain. In some parts of western New York, like Genesee County, enlisted militiamen brought a tradition from New England of electing their non-commissioned officers, lieutenants, and captains.[103] Daniel's company was in a regiment of the militia from Genesee County, reporting to Lieutenant Colonel Alexander Rae.[104]

Although Daniel continued to perform his civic and family duties, perhaps looking toward the future for his three children– Naomi, four; Alfred, three; and Asher one–he got involved in

---

[102] Ellicott spent the years 1798–1800 living outdoors in summer and winter, laying out the townships of the new land in order to complete the Great Survey of the land in October 1800. He surveyed the new city of Washington D.C., was at the Council of Big Tree in 1797, and settling in Batavia, was land agent for 21 years for the Holland Land Company. Chazanof, *Joseph Ellicott and the Holland Land Company: The Opening of Western New York*, 214.
[103] Strum, *"New York Militia and Opposition to the War of 1812"*, 115.
[104] *Military minutes of Council of Appointment 1783-1821.*

improving the school. There had been a log schoolhouse since 1801 on the south side of the Great Genesee Road just east of the creek. At a community meeting, the citizens formed a joint stock company, chaired by Daniel Davis, of which there were 30 shares at $4 each, of which one-half could be paid in labor, produce, or building materials. Mr. Piatt donated the land, the location now occupied by Trigon Park. There they built the first framed schoolhouse west of Genesee River in 1804[105] on the site of the present Methodist parsonage.

"The first newspapers published [in western New York] were the Ontario Gazette and Western Repository, issued from Canandaigua in 1804"[106] the same year Ganson's settlement had its first postmaster, Asher Bates, who was also the sheriff. The postmaster and sheriff's father, Phineas Bates, weekly passed through the settlement on the Niagara Road riding between Canandaigua and Fort Niagara carrying the mail on horseback. The Bates farm was adjacent to the Davises, so perhaps James Sr. walked next door and picked up copies of the newspaper to resume reading the news as he did in Killingworth, by his age, hopefully having turned over much of the farmwork to his sons.

Although on the frontier, the Davises may have had access to an early library in Big Springs, a one hour walk from their farm. "The general intelligence of the citizens of all of the old town of Caledonia, has been proverbial; they enjoyed the benefits of a well selected library, as early as 1804, the Pioneer Library, first west of the Genesee River. The first books were bought at Myron Houey's bookstore, in Canandaigua, by John Garbutt, who carried them to their destination on his back. Peter Shaeffer was the first Librarian. The library now [1851] consists of over 1500 volumes."[107]

---

[105] Beers, 483.
[106] Beers, 501.
[107] Turner, History of the Pioneer Settlement, 499.

Michael A. Ponzio

CHAPTER VII: 1805-1806

By the spring of 1805, Daniel had likely made the final payments he owed for the six lots, perhaps clearing enough forest to be cultivating at least thirty acres. The soil was richer than in Connecticut, allowing him to add the cash crops of wheat and tobacco besides corn and flax. His wife probably supervised their daughter Naomi, five, who took care of their raised bed garden, with Alfred under her watch pulling weeds. Common vegetables could have included Dutch long orange carrots, cabbages, and long scarlet radishes.

Likely they produced a surplus of wheat for sale. The grain was also used as a sort of currency, even accepted to help pay off land loans. A settler who farmed a few miles north of the Davises was recorded in O. Turner's *History of the Pioneer Settlement,* "In 1808, I took wheat to Canandaigua: there was no price and no sale for it there; no exchanging of it for store trade. I removed it to Geneva, at a cost of 12 1/2 cents per bushel, and paid a debt I owed there for a barrel of whiskey with it; the wheat finally netting me 12 1/2 cents per bushel, or one gallon of whiskey for six bushels of wheat."[108]

---

[108] Turner, 503.

Most tobacco was grown for home use, with surpluses sold for cash. Did Daniel smoke cigars? Perhaps he had acquired the habit in Connecticut. "By 1770, cigar smoking had caught on in New England. Cigars were cheap and almost entirely homemade 'paste cigars' so called because the wrapper was glued closed. These were generally rolled by farm wives. Cigars were sold by their husbands or traded to local merchants or Yankee wagon peddlers."[109] And apparently the soil and climate in New York was good to grow tobacco. "In 1786, explorer Sebastian Cobb reported [the Iroquois nation of] Cayuga Indians growing 60 acres of tobacco near present day Elmira, NY. The area between Elmira and Binghamton became a significant cigar-tobacco region called *Big Flats*."[110]

It is likely that the Davises brought a plow with them when they migrated to Ganson's settlement. In 1800, the most commonly used soil tiller was the 'bull plow,' also simply referred to as a 'wooden plow,' because the shaped part that lifts and turns the soil, the mouldboard, was hewed from a tree, although a strip of iron was attached to the 'landside' or bottom to resist wear. If Daniel's plow had worn out or broken, he probably could have replaced it a few miles east of the nearby village of Hartford (present-day Avon) where "Thomas Wiard, a blacksmith and farmer, manufactured bull plows, founding the Wiard Plow Company in 1806."[111] Several years earlier, a plow made of iron had been invented, but perhaps the farmers of western New York were a superstitious lot. "Charles Newbold of Burlington County, New Jersey received a patent for a cast-iron plow in 1797. However, American farmers mistrusted the

---

[109] Hyman, "History of Cigars".
[110] Ibid.
[111] Beers, Gazetteer and Biographical Source, 242.

plow. They believed it "poisoned the soil" and fostered the growth of weeds."[112]

In 1805, Daniel Davis was promoted to the rank of major as commander of a battalion in Alex Reyes's brigade.[113] Daniel began as a lieutenant in 1801, was promoted to captain of his own company, commanding 80 to 100 militiamen in 1803, and now, two years later, chosen as major of a battalion of four companies, about 400 infantrymen. The large number of immigrants arriving in Genesee County[114] had added to the ranks of the militia. By law, white men between the ages of eighteen and forty-five had to enlist.

It may have been the Davises' turn to host the militia training in 1805. "Everybody went to general training, men, women, children, and dogs. Some went on foot, some on horseback, and some in ox-wagons. General training was usually regarded as a pleasant occasion to meet friends, and the boys were provided with a few pennies to buy the inevitable gingerbread. The sale of intoxicating liquors on the ground could only be carried on by permission of the [commanding] officer. Total abstinence was not the rule, however."[115] Daniel Davis ran a public house[116] on the north side of the road and would have made hard cider available to the spectators and the militiamen, hopefully after their training was completed. It would have been convenient for him to buy his supply of fruit stock for fermentation just down the Niagara Road, in east Bloomfield, the next village past Hartford. A variety of apples known as Northern Spy, which is

---

[112] Bellis, "History of the Plow."
[113] Military Minutes of the Council of Appointment:1783-1821.
[114] County population was 1,084 in 1800, Beers, 457, and 12,588 in 1810, *Population of New York State by county.*
[115] Beers, 200.
[116] Britannica, "public house, byname pub, an establishment providing alcoholic beverages to be consumed on the premises".

still grown and used for hard cider making today, was first planted in 1800.[117]

Daniel Davis was major for just one year, promoted to colonel when "in 1806, the militia was erected [organized] into a brigade and the brigade divided into three regiments. Lieutenant Colonel Daniel Davis was appointed commandment in one."[118] Daniel's responsibility had increased, now commanding up to a thousand infantrymen.[119] The general training for the militia was usually conducted over a two-day period each year at the farmstead of the Gansons or at the Davis farm at Limerock, but also on the banks of the Oatka.[120]

For the first couple of years the Davises lived on their new farmstead, they likely visited the Gansons frequently, one of their few neighbors, possibly joining in husking corn, threshing, harvesting, and other communal chores to show goodwill. Most likely, the Gansons returned the favor, and perhaps John and his sons John Jr. and James became close friends with Daniel. "James Ganson was a second Lieutenant in the regiment of Genesee County under Daniel Davis who was Lieutenant Colonel."[121] John Ganson, Jr., and Benjamin Ganson, James's brothers, were likely privates in the same regiment.

John Ganson, Sr., from Bennington, Vermont, had fought in the American Revolution, losing a finger shot off at the Battle of Bunker Hill.[122] He was approaching sixty by 1806 and likely wasn't enlisted, but he was available to advise Daniel Davis with the militia. Ganson had been a captain in General Sullivan's 1788

---

[117] Chaisson, "The Fabled History of Apples".
[118] Military Minutes.
[119] Colonels were chosen by the captains and subalterns of their regiments, and these latter by the written ballots of their respective regiments and separate battalions., Beers, 200.
[120] Ibid., 456.
[121] Ibid.
[122] Cole, The Old Northwest Genealogical Quarterly, 84.

campaign in upstate New York against the Iroquois who had sided with the British. After the war, remembering the fertility of western New York, he returned with his two oldest sons, John Jr., 14, and James, 12, seeking good land to farm. He returned to Vermont to bring back his wife and family, leaving his sons with "a friendly Seneca," so as not to subject his sons to the hardship of the trip again. He was delayed, however, because his wife was sick, lingering for several months before she died in Vermont. He gathered his remaining family and possessions to return to settle on the Genesee River and found his sons quite content living with the Senecas. Could this have been at the Seneca village of Canawaugus, 12 miles down the road from Ganson's settlement?

"This early experience of the Gansons with the Senecas was not without its future use in their intercourse with the tribe, who in large numbers still made this part their camping-ground and council fires. They were always after on a friendly footing with the tribe, and from their knowledge of the language were often called upon as interpreters."[123] A few years later, Ganson moved his family near Oatka Creek to farm and run a tavern. A Quaker missionary staying at his tavern "returning from Niagara mentioned that the number of Indians hanging about such frontier taverns as Ganson's during the winter months made them very disagreeable stations for travelers."[124]

Cornplanter, from nearby Canawaugus, Red Jacket, and other Seneca leaders had visited Ganson's tavern, providing the chance for Daniel to interact with them. Did the exposure influence Daniel's viewpoint of Native Americans? Several years later, in 1813, fugitives from an Iroquois village attacked by the British and their Native American allies were welcomed to camp at the Davises' farm and other farms at Limerock and were given food

---

[123] Beers, 451.
[124] Belluscio, "Ganson's Tavern".

and aid. In addition, the following year, Daniel would fight alongside Red Jacket and the Senecas against the British at the Battle of Fort Erie.

In 1806, Simon Pierson arrived with his family in Ganson's settlement. Like most able-bodied men, he was in the militia and after training in Daniel's brigade for a few years was appointed as quartermaster in 1809.[125] He was an author and wrote in 1856: "In October, 1806, in company with my brother, the late Reverend Josiah Pierson, of Bergen, and our families, I started from Killingworth, Connecticut, with a wagon load of household goods, bound for the Genesee country, 'Where nothing dwelt but beasts of prey, Or men as wild and fierce as they'. Arriving at Ganson's settlement, now LeRoy, we found friends who advised us not to purchase land 'down in the north woods,' for, said they, 'it will always be sickly there; and the region will never be settled.' But having a brother and brother-in-law at Fort Hill, who had preceded us a few months, we resolved upon going there."[126] Thus, Simon ignored their advice and purchased land in the Triangle Tract, a few miles north of present-day LeRoy, near Daniel's brother-in-law, Philemon Nettleton. Simon continued to serve and fought in the War of 1812, likely in the Battle of Fort Erie in Daniel Davis's regiment. He was three years younger than Daniel, and they may have been close friends. He attended Daniel's funeral, writing an account which showed his admiration for Mr. Davis. "It was a very painful scene witnessing the brave man in his coffin . . . he was buried with military honors."

Simon Pierson's words showed the utmost respect for Daniel. And the remembrance of General Davis's bravery was passed through generations of the Ganson family, because in 1875, Dr. Holton Ganson, the son of John Ganson, Jr., had "in his will a

---

[125] Military Minutes. 1064.
[126] Turner, History of Pioneer Settlement, 552.

provision for the erection of a monument to General Davis, of LeRoy at a cost of $550."[127]

---

[127] By the terms of his will his whole estate was to be given to charitable objects in Batavia, viz.: $1,000 to each of the Christian churches, and the remainder to a hospital to be afterwards established. Unfortunately, the Doctor wrote his own will, and not being accustomed to that kind of business failed to comply with some legal requirements necessary to its validity. The will was set aside, and the property distributed according to law. There was in the will also a provision for the erection of a monument, at a cost of $550, to General Davis, of LeRoy. Beers, 67.

Michael A. Ponzio

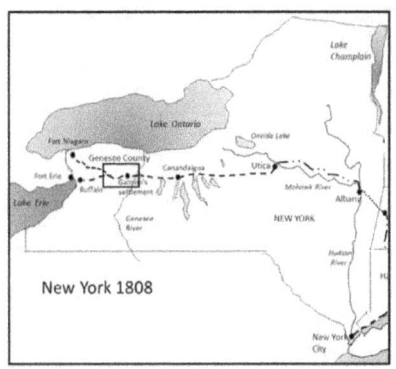

New York 1808

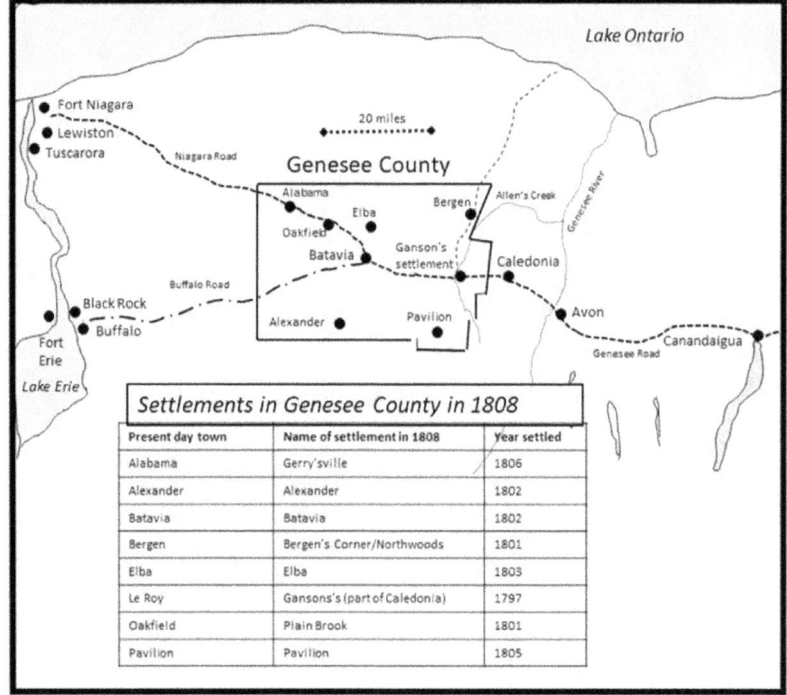

Settlements in Genesee County in 1808

Present day town	Name of settlement in 1808	Year settled
Alabama	Gerry'sville	1806
Alexander	Alexander	1802
Batavia	Batavia	1802
Bergen	Bergen's Corner/Northwoods	1801
Elba	Elba	1803
Le Roy	Gansons's (part of Caledonia)	1797
Oakfield	Plain Brook	1801
Pavilion	Pavilion	1805

Created by Michael A. Ponzio © 2022

CHAPTER VIII: 1807-1810

The Davises may have fully developed the 100 acres on Lot 26 they owned north of the road by 1807. In John Samson's 1929 *History of Brigadier General Daniel Davis,* compiled from local sources, Simon Pierson, who knew Daniel, wrote in 1856, "Daniel Davis who lived on and owned the farm where his father lived, built a frame house in 1807. James Davis Jr. lived on the opposite [south] side of the road."[128] James Jr.; his wife, Jehannah; and two children, Lewis, seven, and Eden, two, had then moved to Lot 13 which the family owned on the south side of the road. (See Chapter V.) James Jr. and Jehannah remained at their new homestead for many years, James passing in 1826 and his wife still living there in 1856. Simon Pierson had also observed in 1806 that Daniel's parents, "an aged couple," were living on the north side of the road on the farm, with their [adult] children, James, Daniel, Norton, Calvin, and Lydia. There are no historical references to Daniel's parents after that year. His

---

[128] Samson, *"History of Brigadier Daniel Davis, Recollections of Simon Pierson".*

father James Sr. would have been about sixty. By 1807, were Daniel's parents deceased?

The first cemetery in present day LeRoy, which "opened about 1801, was on a lot donated for this purpose by Capt. Jotham Curtis, one of the early settlers and a tavern-keeper, on his farm two miles east of the village, and where a Mr. Wiley, the first person whose death is recorded, was buried, subsequently sold to Capt. Daniel Buell, and since known as the Buell farm. This for many years was the sole burying ground."[129] The farm was next to Mud Creek about a mile west of the Davises. The site was known as Limerock Cemetery and eventually Buell Cemetery. Tombstone inscriptions show that Daniel Davis, James Davis Jr. and his son Lewis and wife Mary Ann Bovee Davis, were buried at Buell Cemetery, but there are no records of James Sr. or his wife Hannah. The community did not use any other cemeteries before 1810 and none of them have a record of the parents' burial. The Buell Cemetery was closed for new burials in 1923. Weathering had taken its toll and several of the engravings on the tombstones are illegible. Likely, the family buried Daniel's parents on their own land or at the Buell Cemetery.

That Daniel had the funds to construct a "modern" frame house and James Jr. moved onto additional land across the street showed the Davises had made progress financially in just several years at Limerock. Hopefully, this provided James Sr. and Hannah more comfortable later years and time to enjoy their six grandchildren. By 1807, James Jr. and Jehannah had two children, the oldest son, Lewis, turning seven that year and their second son, Eden, was three. Daniel and Naomi had four children—Naomi, seven; Alfred, six; Asher, four; and Cynthia,

---

[129] Beers,455.

two–making the move by the James Jr. family timely for the growing Davis clan.

As more settlers arrived, they established new hamlets and villages in Southampton township, where Ganson's settlement was located. With the increased population, in 1807, a district comprising Big Springs and Ganson's settlement was partitioned from Southampton. The Scottish settlers of Big Springs named the new township Caledonia, the Latin name the Romans had used for Scotland. The residents within Caledonia continued to call their hamlets Ganson's settlement, Limerock, Big Springs, and Fort Hill.

One of the newer communities in Genesee County was the village of Alexander, founded in 1802 and named after Daniel's senior officer and commander of the Genesee County brigade, General Alexander Rea. In 1808, the general selected the village as the location to conduct the annual training for the new regiment of militia under Lt. Colonel William Rumsey. Because "all the officers of each regiment or battalion were required to rendezvous two days in succession, in June, July, or August, for drill under the brigade inspector,"[130] perhaps the officers of the other regiments of Rea's brigade gathered to observe, assist, and critique the 164th Regiment of Lt. Colonel Rumsey. Lt. Colonel Daniel Davis, who was commander of the 77th Regiment, and Lt. Colonel Asa Ransom, who commanded the 31st infantry regiment of Rea's brigade, would have also been at the training. In addition, the Davises' neighbors, James Ganson, who had been promoted to 2nd Major, and his younger brother, Benjamin Ganson, now Adjutant, were likely at the officers' gathering.

The militiamen of the new regiment likely had arrived with their own weapons, a variety of shotguns, rifles, and muskets. Davis's men had been organized seven years earlier, so possibly

---

[130] Beers, 200.

by 1808 they might have been issued some regulation weapons. "The militia often used the same weapons as regular troops. The main weapon for American foot soldiers was the Springfield Model 1795 Musket, with a 15-inch bayonet. By 1808, regiments of riflemen were provided the U.S. Model 1803 Rifle, manufactured at the Harper's Ferry Armory. The rifles were flintlock, 0.54-inch caliber, and 32 inches long. No bayonet was provided with this rifle, giving the soldiers a major disadvantage in close combat."[131]

Were Daniel's infantrymen issued bayonets? Later in the battles of the Niagara campaign in the War of 1812, American regulars are described as making bayonet charges, but during the Battle of Fort Erie, there is an account of Daniel's brigade under assault after they had captured an enemy battery. "When the British counterattacked—the falling rain and intervening woods screened them until at close quarters, when they [the British] plied the bayonet with deadly effect upon the disorderly crowd of fugitives [retreating Americans], whose arms had been generally rendered unserviceable by the rain."[132] Here, it appears Davis's militia did not have bayonets.

A veteran observer of the 1808 training wrote: "The militiamen [of Rumsey's regiment] armed themselves with old flintlock muskets, horsemen's carbines, long-squirrel rifles, double-barreled shotguns, but wore new 'fine' shirts, about as fine and white as stuff now used for bags, but which cost six shillings per yard, and these were the first fine shirts worn in this town."[133]

---

[131] Howell, *"Weapons in the War of 1812."*
[132] Cruikshank, *The Siege of Fort Erie, August 1st-September 23rd, 1814*, 37.
[133] Beers, 200.

Sometime after September 1808, Daniel Davis was initiated into the Freemasons at the Avon, New York, Lodge No. 130, chartered February 13, 1806.[134] Why did Daniel join the Masons? He was involved in his community during his first eight years in Genesee County, serving as pathmaster, school board member, militia officer, and operator of a tavern on Niagara Road. Did he want to be a Freemason for social contacts, or did he identify with the Freemasons' principles?

Amid the *Second Great Awakening*, people were not only being "freed" of the grip of the Congregational church by the evangelical preachers, but many adopted the ideas from the *Enlightenment*, which spread the concepts of free thinking, anti-royalism, republicanism, and constitutional government. The ideas were popular among the ranks of the writers and signers of the United States Declaration of Independence and the Constitution, including George Washington and Benjamin Franklin.

"By the late 18th century, at the height of the *Enlightenment*, Freemasonry carried considerable social cachet. Being a Mason signaled that you were at the forefront of knowledge."[135] Freemasonry "became a social phenomenon to join. For men of good character, men seeking to rise in society, men from all walks of life, it was a thing to do."[136]

The Freemasons held three principles that may have attracted Daniel to join. These consisted of following the brotherhood of man ("Golden Rule"), charity, and truth. Officially, members were accepted from any religion or lack of religion but were

---

[134] Samson, *History of Daniel Davis, Extracts from a letter of the Grand Secretary Robert Kenworthy, Jan.18, 1930.*
[135] Harland-Jacobs, *Handbook of Freemasonry*, 439.
[136] Tabbert, *"Freemasonry in Colonial America"*. [136] Beers, 200.
[136] Samson, *History of Daniel Davis, Extracts from a letter of the Grand Secretary Robert Kenworthy, Jan.18, 1930.*
[136] Harland-Jacobs, *Handbook of Freemasonry*, 439.

"encouraged to believe in a supreme being, which in the parlance of Masonry, is known as the 'Grand Architect of the Universe.'"[137]

For several years, Daniel Davis likely rode the fourteen miles east to Avon, attending the Freemason meetings. In 1811, the Olive Branch Lodge, No. 39, was chartered[138] in Batavia, the meetings held at various public taverns. The new lodge was thirteen miles in the opposite direction from Avon. Perhaps Daniel attended the meetings in Batavia, or at both locations.

In 1810, a newcomer arrived in Ganson's settlement who would significantly contribute to the community as well as be influential in Daniel's life. "Dr. William Sheldon came originally from Rupert, Vermont. Born in 1788, he came to the Genesee country on horseback in 1810. He had very little money and only a few medical instruments in his saddlebags, including a lancet for bloodletting and a turnkey for extracting teeth. He stopped at the Ganson Inn, not knowing how he would pay for his room and board. But Mrs. Ganson was ill, and Dr. Sheldon treated her in exchange for his bill."[139]

Dr. Sheldon married the widow of the late postmaster, Asher Bates, and lived with her on her farm, next to Daniel Davis's homestead. Sheldon also became a Freemason in the Olive Branch lodge, joined the militia, and was a surgeon holding the rank of captain reporting to Daniel Davis. Sheldon became aide-de-camp to Daniel Davis, who had been promoted to full colonel in 1809. As the colonel's confidential assistant, Sheldon and Davis certainly developed a close relationship.

---

[137] Harland-Jacobs, 439.
[138] Beers, 233.
[139] Belluscio, Lynne, *June 8, 1812-2012, Our Bicentennial.*

Brigadier General Daniel Davis and the War of 1812

In 1807, a war across the Atlantic between Napoleonic France and Great Britain had an adverse impact on Western New York. British warships were illegally stopping American merchant vessels at sea, searching for war material they suspected was being sent to Britain's enemy. The British were also boarding United States merchant ships on the high seas, seizing American sailors, claiming they were English deserters or citizens, and impressing the captives, forcibly making them serve in their navy. President Jefferson retaliated by prompting Congress to pass the Embargo Act of 1807, which restricted trade with England.

Indicative of Daniel Davis's modest prosperity, he likely earned cash from selling wheat. Brokers bought the surplus grain from successful farmers on the New York frontier. Teamsters delivered the product via wagon on the improved Seneca Turnpike to Utica, transferred the wheat to bateaux to float down the Mohawk River to Albany, where it was loaded onto sloops bound for New York City. "Europe provided the major market for New York's surplus grain."[140] The disruption in trade would directly impact Daniel Davis's livelihood.

The British, as if preparing for war, bolstered their arsenals and had improved the fortifications along the Niagara River in Canada. In 1810, President James Madison's request for funds to increase the size of the army and equip a large volunteer force was denied by Congress. Instead, the federal government notified the governor of New York to put their militia on alert status and gave the president the right to call up other state militias. "When rumors of war began to agitate the country, the [New York] State authorities contracted with Joseph Ellicott [Holland Land Co. agent] to build an arsenal. He erected one of

---

[140] Strum, *"New York Federalists and Opposition to the War of 1812."*, 170.

logs, 20 feet square, at the forks of the road in Batavia [south fork to Buffalo and north fork to Fort Niagara]."[141]

Perhaps the militia training in 1810 was in Batavia, the county seat of Genesee County, which had 56 settlers in 1802, about 1,000 in 1809, and by 1810 had 3,610 inhabitants, the largest town west of the Genesee River. Dr. Sheldon had joined the militia. Another doctor in the militia from the community was Dr. Frederick Fitch, who had begun practice in 1808 in Ganson's settlement. "He was of an eccentric character, and fond of military display. On an occasion of general training, wishing to display his skill in sword exercise, he wounded himself in the leg, which resulted in requiring an amputation of the limb."[142] Perhaps Dr. Sheldon was present at the incident, which would have been very fortunate for Dr. Fitch. Certainly, his days in the militia were over, but apparently, he was capable of continuing his physician's practice. The community considered Dr. Fitch a skillful practitioner and he later formed a partnership with Dr. Sheldon.

---

[141] Beers, 202.
[142] Ibid, 473.

Brigadier General Daniel Davis and the War of 1812

Michael A. Ponzio

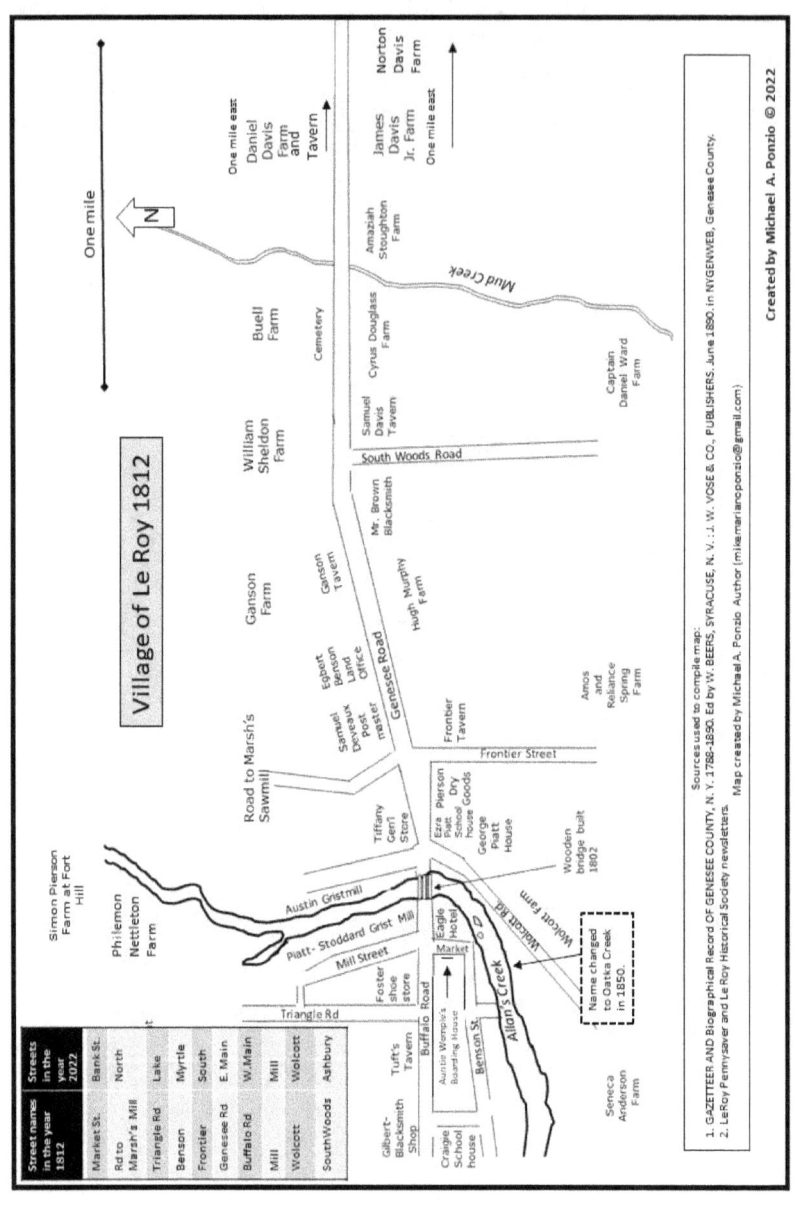

CHAPTER IX: The War of 1812 Begins

By 1811 Ganson's settlement had grown into a sizable community, with several grist mills, four or five taverns, a couple of blacksmiths, general mercantile stores, and even a hotel. The new businesses had located west of the creek. The Davises were among the 2,355 inhabitants recorded in the 1810 federal census for Caledonia township.[143]

Perhaps Daniel Davis no longer had to wait two weeks for the newspaper to be delivered from Canandaigua, forty-five miles by postriders. Since 1807, he may have been reading more up-to-date news in the *Cornucopia,* published in nearby Batavia, only sixteen miles from his farm. He might have persuaded regular customers traveling between Batavia and Caledonia, stopping at his tavern, to drop off recent editions, perhaps along with friendly conversation and a gratuitous hard cider for the favor. The *Cornucopia* ceased printing in 1811, but it was quickly replaced by a new publication, the *Republican Advocate*. After acquiring an edition of the *Advocate* on December 16, 1811, perhaps Daniel read about the Battle of Tippecanoe. On the northwest frontier, Shawnee Chief Tecumseh and his brother, a spiritual leader, *The Prophet*, who made use of religious visions to

---

[143] Beers, 662.

attract loyal followers, had been organizing a confederacy of Native American tribes to halt the encroachment on their land. General William Harrison, the governor of Indiana Territory, perceived the confederacy as an impending threat. While Tecumseh was absent recruiting more allies, Harrison launched a preemptive attack, destroying the confederacy's main village in northern Indiana. Likely Daniel didn't feel threatened by the event which occurred over five hundred miles away. However, he may have sensed that the spiritual teachings of Tecumseh's brother were similar to a new movement spreading among the Seneca by a nearby religious sachem named Handsome Lake.[144] The Canawaugus Seneca village was barely ten miles from his farm. Daniel's neighbors, the Gansons, however, had many years of friendly relations with the Senecas, which possibly helped keep the peace with them.

Instead of ending the threat from the Native Americans, Harrison's attack drove Tecumseh to form an alliance with the British. The battle also influenced more tribes to join the restored Tecumseh confederacy, including the Mohawk Iroquois, just across the Niagara River in Canada, an immediate threat to the Davises.

Daniel finished the article, perhaps for a fleeting moment wondering if the Seneca's new religion would become militant, then his attention turned to a notice that "the bounty for a wolf hide, which was $1" when he arrived in western New York, "had increased to $10 per hide, such was the havoc of the wolves among the herds."[145] He may have glanced at several columns of advertisements by the Holland Land Company and noticed land prices had increased to $16 per acre. Perhaps he smiled as he

---

[144] The half-brother of Complanter, Handsome Lake (1735 – 1815), became the "prophet" of a regenerated Indian "religion" which still has many followers. Seneca Indian Country Historical Marker.
[145] Beers, 466.

thought about the three dollars per acre he had paid in 1800. By 1811, he had made substantial progress on his homestead, erecting a larger frame house. He might have converted his late parents' cabin into a tavern. His older brother, James Jr., was likely thriving across the road and hopefully so was younger brother, Norton, a few lots east.

As Daniel continued to read his newspaper, perhaps he suddenly felt the ground move, the cups and plates on the tables rattle, and dust sprinkle down from the rafters. There were shouts from people outside. It was a mystery what had happened until weeks later, an issue of the *Advocate* in January 1812 explained that Daniel had experienced the distant rumblings of an earthquake from southeast Missouri near the Mississippi River. People all over the eastern U.S., including President Madison in Washington D.C., had felt the ground move. The shaking even rang church bells in Boston. The massive earthquake destroyed towns and thousands of acres of forests, but the most fantastic tale was that watermen on flatboats reported the Mississippi River had temporarily run backwards.

Certainly, by word-of-mouth from travelers and the newspapers sprouting up across western New York by 1812, Daniel Davis was learning of the world events that affected his community. A complex system of trade embargos was plunging the American economy into recession. Britain, still at war, tried to restrict overseas trade between the United States and her enemy, France. France did the same. The British navy continued to impress[146] American sailors into their navy, and the raids on white settlements by Tecumseh's confederacy, encouraged by the British, grew closer to western New York.

---

[146] Estimates are from 6,000 (Smithsonian Inst.) to 15,000 (PBS) sailors claiming they were American citizens, who were forced to serve on British warships.

There were fierce rhetorical battles in Congress for and against declaring war on Britain. The Federalists were opposed to war, mostly in support of New England, whose economy heavily depended on international trade. The "war hawks" of the Republican Party were dominant in the western and southern states, especially on the frontiers, most affected by the attacks from the Native Americans. The war hawks also saw the opportunity for expansion by invading and acquiring Canada and Florida.

In June 1812, the British Parliament rescinded the trading law harmful to the United States. Two days later, on June 16, and at the insistence of President Madison, without knowledge of this repeal, Congress declared war against Britain. (It took about a month for news to travel by sailing ship from England to the United States.) The country's opinions were divided on the decision. There were riots in Baltimore, New York, and Washington, by anti-war and pro-war elements.

While the United States eastern seaboard was in turmoil, the people of western New York dreaded the possibility of attacks, incited by the British, from local Senecas, as well as the thousands of Iroquois allied to Britain who lived in Canada. There was also fear of invasion by British armies across the Niagara River. Certainly, Daniel Davis, as commander of the 77th regiment, met with his officers to ensure readiness of the militia. On June 8, 1812, the State Legislature voted to divide the town of Caledonia; the west part, Ganson's Settlement, would become the town of Bellona,[147] the east side would retain the name Caledonia. To update the rosters due to the revision of the township boundaries, Daniel likely met with the captains of his regiment, who were responsible for the muster roles of their respective companies.

---

[147] Bellona was the Roman goddess of war.

Brigadier General Daniel Davis and the War of 1812

By August, when President Madison finally learned of the favorable news on the trading issues, the British had already captured two American outposts on the northwest frontier at Fort Dearborn (present day Chicago) and Fort Mackinac. Then later in August 1812, a series of battles ensued as the American attempt to invade Canada failed, ending with a counterattack by British forces allied with Tecumseh and his warriors, forcing the Americans to surrender Detroit.

Within a month of the failure at Detroit, the Americans began planning a second attempt to invade Canada, this time across the Niagara River, making it likely the New York militia would be mustered for duty. Daniel may have wondered if his Genesee County brigade would be called up. He must have been aware of the refusal of the New York militia from the Hudson Valley and New York City to muster for the war. Even closer to home, the "militiamen of Chautauqua County, south of Buffalo, ignored the call-up by Stephen Van Rensselaer, the commander of the state militia."[148]

Congress ratified the declaration of war by a narrow margin, as the war hawk Republicans outvoted the Federalists. Major opposition to the war persisted nationwide. "Under the New York state constitution, the militia was a defensive force, and militiamen did not have to participate in offensive operations requiring an invasion of Canada. Men serving in the militia expected to protect their families, their communities, and New York, and did not expect to invade Canada. Throughout the war Federalists hammered away at this point, and repeatedly discouraged militiamen, Federalists and Republicans from engaging in offensive operations."[149]

Daniel Davis certainly must have made plans with his family for his expected absence if called up. "Militia service was limited

---

[148] Strum, *"New York Federalists and Opposition to the War of 1812."*, 172.
[149] Ibid., 115.

to three months per year, beyond which volunteers were not obligated to stay. Units would be formed and released but then general orders would be issued to raise another local unit to go to the front. Local soldiers primarily served on the Niagara Frontier, but some were sent to villages along Lake Ontario to defend against British raids."[150]

During the summer of 1812, Daniel, living alongside the only road that spanned western New York, likely observed the first regiments of militia file by on their way to the Niagara Frontier. "Soldiers were marched to LeRoy, thence to Buffalo and Lewiston, because there were no other land routes."[151] Brigadier General William Wadsworth, in command of the 7th Brigade, New York State Militia, assumed the order to deliver the regiments from the counties of Seneca, Cayuga, and Ontario to Black Rock to reinforce federal troops for the invasion of Upper Canada. Wadsworth started with his brigade in Canandaigua and trooped by Daniel's farm on the Genesee Road, perhaps resting his men during the long march at the roadhouses, including Daniel's tavern, to quench their thirst.

Major General Stephen Van Rensselaer took command of the 6,000 regular and militia forces at Black Rock. At dawn on October 13, 1812, the first wave of 1,300 Americans crossed the Niagara River in small boats, taking the heights above the village of Queenston. A counterattack by the British regulars, Canadian militia, and Mohawk allies, however, pinned the Americans with their backs to the cliffs they had just scaled overlooking the river. Now daylight, the second wave of Americans failed to cross when the British artillery shattered their boats. Lt. Colonel Winfield Scott, leading the regulars, and Brigadier General Wadsworth, the militia, sent for reinforcements still across the

---

[150] War-of-1812-panels-for-web.pdf (historicgeneva.org)
[151] Beers, 35.

river. "The New York State militias were watching the battle from the American shore. They witnessed the death and destruction firsthand. They also saw the results as the dead and injured Americans were ferried back across the river. When the time came for them to join their regular American army counterparts on the Canadian side of the river, they refused to go, which under their constitution they had the right to do."[152]

By late afternoon, the Americans were low on ammunition; the militia commander, Wadsworth, was wounded; and without reinforcements, they surrendered. About thirty combatants on the British side were killed, with American fatalities ten times greater plus 1,000 were taken prisoner. After the disastrous Battle of Queenston Heights, both Van Rensselaer and Wadsworth resigned. A month later the New York militia contingent of an American force attempting to invade Lower Canada and attack Montreal refused to cross the border. The excursion failed.

What was Daniel Davis's reaction when he learned of the militia's poor showing at Queenston and Montreal? Aaron Tufts, a militiaman in Daniel's brigade, recalled comments after word spread that the British taunted that the American militia would not fight. Daniel's retort was that "he would show the British and the world that the militia dare fight." [153]

---

[152] *"Niagara Falls History, the Battle of Queenston Heights".*
[153] Tufts, *"Some Reminisces from the Past".*

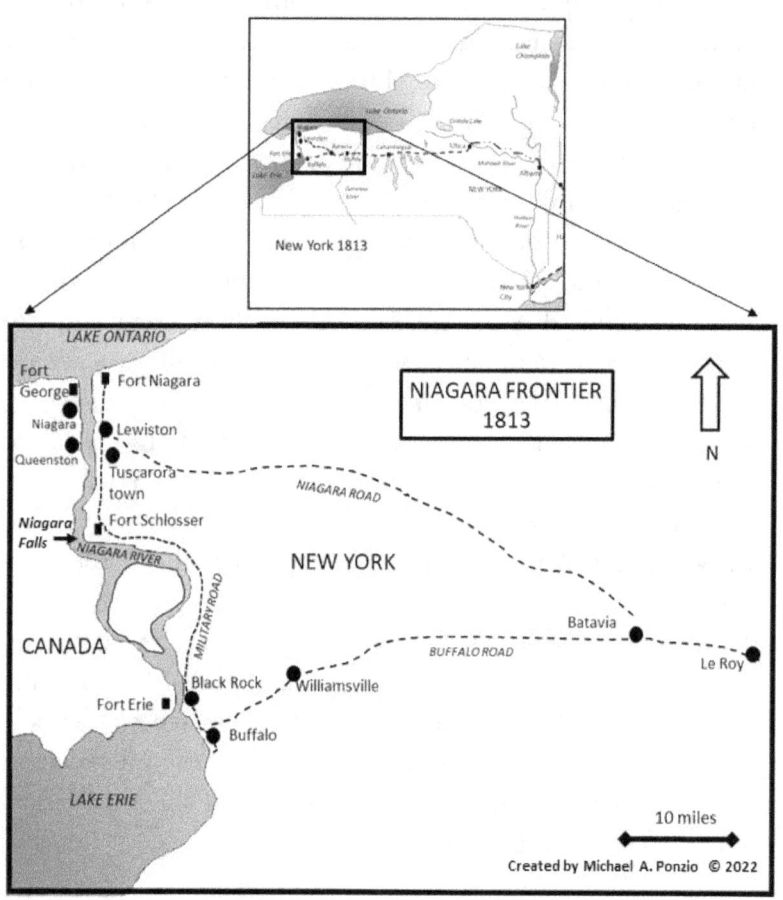

CHAPTER X: 1813

During 1812, the United States had lost most of the land engagements of the war, including the disastrous Battle of Queenston Heights. The flood of new settlers to western New York slowed, then halted by 1813. Gone were the American war hawk claims as expressed by Senator Henry Clay in his address to Congress, that "the Kentucky militia alone are competent to lay Montreal and Upper Canada at the feet of the United States."[154] The year culminated with no significant action on the Niagara Frontier, leaving Daniel Davis and most of the militiamen in Genesee County home for the harvest.

The bright news for the Americans was the victories at sea in duels against British warships. The *USS Constitution*, one of seven American 44-gun frigates, had been the most successful. American sailors had christened the warship "Old Ironsides" because during a battle on the high seas with the British frigate HMS *Guerriere* the enemy cannon balls had bounced off the *USS*

---

[154] Hall, "Canadian Annexation Sentiment in Kentucky Prior to the War of 1812.", 374. After the American Revolution, many British loyalists emigrated from the U.S. to the British held Province of Quebec, which was then split into two colonies of Lower Canada (French speaking-present day Quebec) and Upper Canada (English speaking-southern portion of present day Ontario).

Constitution's hull. The American frigate was made of live oak harvested in Georgia, which was denser than the oak in England.[155] The *Constitution's* broadsides (a nearly simultaneous firing of all the guns from one side of a warship) destroyed the British ship.

The British Navy, however, the largest in the world, reinforced their fleet off the coasts of the United States. "By early 1813, the British had eleven ships of the line, thirty-four frigates, and fifty-two other vessels operating off North America. They had driven the American frigates back into their ports, resulting in only two U.S. frigates [out of seven] venturing out to sea."[156] The British fleet, using their numerical advantage, established a blockade of American seaports along the coasts of the southern and Atlantic states by November 1813.

Early in 1813, the United States continued to see defeats on land, until a successful amphibious raid in April on York (Toronto). Then in May, U.S. forces seized Fort George at the mouth of the Niagara River. The British forces retreated to Burlington Heights (present day Hamilton), leaving the Americans to occupy all the posts on the Canadian side of the Niagara River: Fort George, Queenston, and Fort Erie. Likely, Daniel's family felt some relief that the Niagara Frontier was more secure, decreasing the threat of invasion and the need for the Genesee militia to be called out.

Although the war front had shifted away from the nearby frontier only sixty miles away, Daniel would have been busy preparing and training in the event his regiment was mustered. A quote from the 1899 North's Gazetteer of Genesee County

---

[155] The navy had hired woodcutters from New England to harvest the live oak in Georgia, but they were not successful, many of them had died from disease. Instead, enslaved workers harvested the most important timbers for the hulls of the early American navy. Herzog, *"Slavery and the USS Constitution"*.
[156] Prom, *The U.S. Navy in the War of 1812:*

asserted, "He had a strong passion for military life and was one of the first to enlist in the War of 1812."[157] It is likely his war duties took precedence over the civic responsibilities he had assumed in his earlier years on the school board and as pathmaster.

Perhaps Daniel's older brother James stepped forward to help. "In 1813, the State Legislature changed the village name Bellona, to LeRoy, named after Herman LeRoy, a wealthy New York City merchant, land speculator, and owner of the Triangle Tract, a portion of which now contains the town."[158] "At the first town meeting of LeRoy on April 6, 1813, Dr. William Sheldon was elected as the town supervisor and James Davis Jr. was elected as one of the Overseers of Highways."[159] James Davis Jr. is not listed in the *Military Minutes of the Council of Appointment: 1783-1821,* which only includes militia officers. So, it is possible he was a private in the militia; however, his role to construct and maintain the roads, especially the bridge over Oatka Creek, must have been a key assignment. All troops and materiel going to the Niagara Frontier traveled on the Genesee Road through LeRoy, the only road to Buffalo, Black Rock, and Fort Niagara. James must have diverted time from his farmwork to keep the roads open to move troops to the frontier, so perhaps his oldest son Lewis, now thirteen, took on more farming tasks. Eden was nine and surely helped him. His youngest child, Ezra, was five, likely caring for their garden.

Across the road, Daniel's wife had her hands full with six children, with the oldest, Naomi, at thirteen, certainly involved in taking care of her siblings, especially Cynthia, eight, and David, six. They all would be doing their share of farm work.

---

[157] Samson, John P., *History of Brigadier Daniel Davis.*
[158] *"Town of LeRoy".*
[159] Samson, *"J.L. Crocker's Scrapbook."*

Michael A. Ponzio

The war returned to the Niagara Frontier in May 1813, with the Americans' capture of Fort George, spearheaded by Winfield Scott's disciplined soldiers. The U.S. Army now controlled the entire Niagara peninsula between Lake Erie and Lake Ontario, but the Americans' advance further into Upper Canada was halted after suffering defeat in two consecutive battles. The Americans retreated, occupying only a small area in the vicinity of Fort George. More New York militia were called up, including a battalion of just under 400 men from Genesee County, commanded by Major Parmenio Adams. His battalion was part of Lt. Colonel Vary's 99th Regiment from Batavia, in the same brigade as the 77th Regiment led by Daniel Davis, which consisted of volunteers from LeRoy.

In the back-and-forth Niagara campaign, on the night of July 10, 1813, the British silently crossed the river, landing at Black Rock, the location of important American military stores and a shipyard. British regulars, outnumbering the Americans two to one, surprised the unprepared Genesee militia, who fled their camp and scattered. Major Adams's aide-de-camp, Lieutenant Phineas Staunton, took command, retreating south, and holding together about 100 of the Genesee militia. He was reinforced by militia from local counties, a company of regulars, and a band of Seneca warriors, coming from Buffalo. The combined force rushed to Black Rock, to find the British had already set fire to several buildings. The Americans counterattacked, inflicting many casualties on the British, as they drove them to their boats, escaping to Canada.

When news of the skirmish reached LeRoy, the local residents would have learned that Seneca warriors had fought alongside the Americans in the battle, which may have eased their concerns about the Native Americans' loyalty at the nearby village of Canawaugus.[160] Also, Daniel Davis probably knew the two officers that commanded the Genesee militia in the battle, certainly having trained with both Lt. Phineas Staunton and Major Parmenio Adams. When their three-month term expired and they returned to Batavia, perhaps Daniel made the short ride, paying them a visit to find out about the battle. Certainly, Daniel was eager to learn about the British methods of warfare.

Crisfield Johnson, a 19th century author of a score of American history books, gives much credit to eyewitnesses as sources for his *History of Erie County*. He wrote, "A great part of this history is derived from *living lips*. I would tender especial thanks for such aid to General William Warren, for nearly seventy years a resident of Erie, whom I visited to consult, and whose memory of the stirring scenes [of the skirmish at Black Rock] in which he took an active part, is hardly dimmed by his ninety-one years of age."[161]

Using General Warren's firsthand eyewitness narrative, imagine a conversation Daniel Davis might have had with Lieutenant Staunton, recounting the Battle of Black Rock. Perhaps they shared a hard cider at a tavern in Batavia with Major Adams. At Daniel's urging, Lt. Staunton described the day months earlier at Black Rock.

"The British column silently approached our encampment. Our men must have been aroused a little before the enemy

---

[160] Many of the younger [Seneca] men hurried west to join the forces of Tecumseh and the prophet, or ally themselves with Little Turtle, the Miami. This bold idea was opposed with vigor by both Red Jacket and Handsome Lake. The latter used his influence to dissuade his converts from having anything to do with the affairs of the western tribes against the Americans. Handsome Lake was a " peace prophet". Parker, *The Senecas in the War of 1812.*

[161] Johnson, *Centennial History of Erie County*, 8.

reached them, for they all made their escape, but they attempted no resistance and fled without even spiking the cannon in their charge. When the militia first began its retreat, Major Adams," Staunton paused, nodding at the major, "sent a messenger to Buffalo. I kept together about 100 of the Genesee militia with me as we carried Major Adams, too ill to walk or ride, and headed toward Buffalo. There, General Porter and Captain Cummings mustered their recruits and marched toward the scene of action. Farmer's Brother, a Seneca chief, over eighty years old, at once gathered his warriors who were placed under the command of Captain William Hull of the militia. Bringing together his forces, numbering but about three hundred, General Porter now felt able to cope with the enemy. Because of the major's supineness, I led the Genesee militia on the left, nearest the river, while Captain Hull's men were with the Indians, who had gathered in the woods on the right front. The militia . . ."

Staunton paused as Major Adams clasped the lieutenant's shoulder and said, "Gallantly led by Lieutenant Staunton!"

Then Staunton may have laughed and continued, "And all of us ashamed of our recent flight, we dashed forward against the enemy. A fight of some fifteen or twenty minutes ensued, in which the militia stood up against the British regulars without flinching, though three of their [our] men were killed and five wounded, no slight loss out of a hundred in so short a time. The right flank of the Americans came up, the Indians raised the war-whoop and opened fire, and it has often been found that the capacity of these painted warriors for inspiring fear is much greater than the actual injury they inflict. The Genesee boys were in the front of the fray throughout and gallantly retrieved their tarnished reputation."

Adams then added, "Their good conduct was doubtless due largely to the example of Adjutant Lt. Staunton, whom I, in my predicament, allowed to take full command. And all the accounts speak in high terms of the conduct of the Seneca warriors. They fought well and were not especially savage."[162]

Another source agrees with the conduct of the Iroquois fighting for the Americans in the war. "The Iroquois agreed to fight under civilized rules and to take no scalps and to murder no captives. This pledge they sacredly kept." [163]

Certainly, Daniel Davis was inspired by his comrades' heroics and stiffened in his determination to show the Genesee militia could defend their homeland. Perhaps he slapped Lt. Staunton on the back for a job well done, then bought him another hard cider and toasted him.

In September 1813, encouraging news reached Daniel, perhaps by word from travelers who stopped at his tavern, or in *The Advocate*, the newspaper from Batavia. Admiral Perry had led the American squadron in a naval victory over the British on Lake Erie, capturing or destroying their entire fleet. The United States now had complete control of the lake, facilitating the recovery of Detroit by General Harrison after a brief fight. His army then crossed the border into Upper Canada to defeat a Canadian army on the Thames River in October. Chief Tecumseh was killed in the battle, severely weakening the Native American confederacy. Attacks on settlements in Ohio and Alabama by native Americans allied to Britain continued as well as duels at sea between American and British warships, but it calmed along the Niagara frontier. The Davises could complete another harvest, hoping for peace.

---

[162] Johnson, *Centennial History of Erie County*, 238.
[163] Parker *"The Senecas in the War of 1812."*, 84.

Michael A. Ponzio

 GENESEE COUNTY MILITIA COMMANDING OFFICERS 1813

7TH Division- Major General Amos Hall (Bloomfield, Ontario County)
6th Brigade- Brigadier General Alexander Rea (Batavia)
31st Regiment- Lt. Colonel John Acheson (Parma)
77th Regiment- Lt. Colonel Daniel Davis (Le Roy)
99th Regiment- Lt. Colonel William Vary (Sheldon)
161st Regiment- Lt. Colonel Mattias Lemen (Williamsburg)
164th Regiment- Lt. Colonel Worth L. Churchill (Bennington)

Source: Genesee County New York History Department
https://www.co.genesee.ny.us/departments/history/war_of_1812.php

CHAPTER XI: Battle of Buffalo, December 1813

By August 1813, the American forces had lost all the territory previously gained on the Canadian side of the river, except for Fort George, which the British harassed and kept under a loose siege. The military commander of the district, Major General James Wilkinson, transferred the regulars from Harrison's army at Detroit and McClure's troops at Fort George, to the east, for a second attempt to invade Lower Canada and take Montreal. When these soldiers marched past his farm, heading east, Daniel must have been concerned that the Niagara Frontier was now lightly defended.

In October, the invasion of Lower Canada at Montreal hundreds of miles to the north failed and was deemed a disaster, although the two-pronged American forces had outnumbered the defenders, mostly French Canadians and Mohawks. The defeated Americans wintered in northern New York, leaving the shipyard at Black Rock and Fort Niagara defended primarily by militia. With this knowledge, the British dispatched a force of regulars to retake Fort George, compelling General McClure to abandon the site. Before he evacuated to the American side of the river, his next decision would affect the lives of thousands of inhabitants of the Niagara region, directly threatening the Davises and impacting Daniel's life a year later.

On a cold, snowy day, December 10, 1813, with only an hour's notice to the 400 Canadian residents to evacuate, McClure ordered the nearby village of Niagara burned.[164] The British condemned this act as being outside the common rules of war. Afterwards, it led to the vindictive counterattacks that followed. Burning the village was widely denounced by the American citizens of western New York.[165]

The British exacted swift revenge on December 18. Five hundred regulars with an equal number of Mohawks crossed the river at night, silently attacking Fort Niagara solely with bayonets, killing sixty of the 400 American soldiers, many of them after they surrendered.[166] The rest were captured. The British regulars, with their Mohawk allies, continued their attacks along the Niagara River, killing soldiers and citizens, looting, and burning the American villages of Youngstown, Fort Schlosser, and Lewiston.

Tuscaroran Chief Elias Johnson wrote in an 1881 history of the Tuscaroras, describing the British attack on Lewiston, "The American citizens of Lewiston, some in bare feet and pajamas, fled through mud and snow. To their rescue, two dozen

---

[164] The village of Newark was established in 1792 as the capital of Upper Canada. The capital was moved to York (Toronto) in 1796, and Newark's name was changed to Niagara, eventually to Niagara-on-the-Lake. Britannica, *"Niagara-on-the-Lake."*

[165] In his defense, McClure publicly released the letter from the Secretary of War, John Armstrong, that he received two months before he burned the village. Armstrong stated: "Sir —Understanding that the defence [sic] of the post committed to your charge may render it proper to destroy the town of [Niagara] N. A. you are hereby directed to apprize its inhabitants of this circumstance, and to invite them to remove themselves and their effects to some place of greater safety." Critics respond stating that McClure was not defending the fort, but only abandoning it and there was no need to burn Niagara. McClure, *"George. Gen. McClure's further relation of facts."*

[166] Barbuto, Lt. Col. Richard V., *"The War of 1812 on the Niagara River".*

Tuscarora Iroquois men ran from their nearby hillside village, firing muskets and screaming war whoops. The British, not knowing how few Tuscaroras there really were and fearing an ambush, halted their pursuit. That bought time for many of the villagers to reach safety. By this time, the train of white people had gone quite a good way in their flight. It is evident that the timely intervention of the Tuscarora Indians saved great slaughter of men, women, and children among the white people."[167]

McClure had left a week before the British had attacked Fort Niagara and had gone south to defend Buffalo. He wrote, "I received by express from Buffalo and Black Rock, petitions and proceedings of meetings of the inhabitants, begging for protection."[168] In a few days, without knowledge of the attack on Fort Niagara, the general then departed Buffalo, taking all the regular troops, and went to Batavia to collect additional militia that had been called out by the governor. McClure learned of the slaughter of the civilians and destruction of the Niagara villages while he was in Batavia. On December 26, the governor replaced McClure for incompetence. His replacement, Major General Amos Hall, led the newly recruited militia to Buffalo. "McClure retired to his home was justly followed by the hatred and contempt of thousands. The destruction of the Niagara frontier is chargeable chiefly to the cruelty and cowardice of George McClure."[169]

What of the people who fled the retaliatory attacks by the British and their Mohawk allies? "The terrified civilians all along the Niagara Frontier fled in the face of the British onslaught. Often times, so great and disorderly was their effort to escape that family members became separated from one another. For

---

[167] *"A Piece of New York State History"*
[168] McClure, *"George. Gen. McClure's further relation of facts."*
[169] Johnson, *Centennial History of Erie County.*

weeks afterwards, the Niagara Frontier remained both deserted and desolate."[170]

"Private homes were thrown open, barns and sheds occupied by refugees, and separated families were reunited. In Batavia, the home of the Holland Land Company's agent, Joseph Ellicott, housed army officers. The Land Office, a wing on Ellicott's mansion, served as a hospital."[171]

The depiction by Frederick W. Beers, editor of the Gazetteer and Biographical Record of Genesee County, N.Y. 1788-1890 is dramatic. "This [escape of the fugitives] occurred in midwinter and the defenceless [sic] inhabitants, including delicate women and young children, were driven into the snow-bound forests to find home and shelter in outlying settlements of the interior. These were cheerfully given, and the rites of hospitality to the houseless sufferers were in no place more cheerfully [sic] accorded than to those who reached LeRoy. Never was hospitality more general or more needed. It was extended to the Tuscaroras, whose cabins had not escaped the British torch. They came to Ganson settlement where they were provided with a camping ground on what is now Lime Rock [sic], three miles east, and were supplied with provisions by the settlers and in part by the commissary of the public stores."[172]

The Tuscaroras, against overwhelming odds, stopped the British and Mohawk attack at Lewiston long enough for the inhabitants to escape. According to the source, they camped at Limerock, possibly at Daniel Davis's or the Ganson's farms. Perhaps the Davises, who owned three farms (Daniel, James Jr., and Norton S.) at Limerock had enough surplus to provide food for the Tuscaroras. It was December. Did they invite them to shelter in their barns? Their neighbors, the Gansons, with their

---

[170] North, *"Descriptive and Biographical Record of Genesee County"*, 135.
[171] Beers, 34.
[172] Ibid., 475.

history of friendship with the Senecas, would likely have provided help and could interpret when needed. Some of the Tuscaroras were Christians who had lost their church in the destruction. Did the people of LeRoy invite them to their Sunday services?

The first wave of war fugitives arrived in LeRoy and Batavia during the last week of December 1813. Batavia became General Amos Hall's base of operations to defend Black Rock, Buffalo, and western New York. By December 27, the general had gathered a force of about 2,000 militia, posting half in Buffalo and the other half a few miles north in Black Rock. Among the militia garrisoned in Black Rock were two companies from the Genesee County 6th Brigade, one from the 164th Regiment led by Lt. Colonel Churchill and the second commanded by Major Adams, after recovering from his illness, leading a battalion from the brigade's 99th Regiment. One of the companies in Major Adams's battalion was led by Dr. William Sheldon, a captain in the militia as well as a military surgeon. He was the close friend and neighbor of Daniel Davis. About one hundred Native American warriors, Senecas, Onondagas, and Oneidas, outraged by the British attack on the Tuscaroras, joined the American forces.[173]

In the dark hours before dawn on December 30, 1813, a force of 500 British regulars and 400 Mohawks crossed the Niagara River, landing near Black Rock, only detected by American patrols after the British had fully disembarked. General Hall, in charge of the American defense, at first thought the landing was

---

[173] The Five Nations, comprised of the Seneca, Cayuga, Onondaga, Oneida, and Mohawk, united in confederation about the year A.D. 1200. Each nation gave its pledge not to war with other members of the confederation. Around 1720, the Tuscarora nation was admitted into the league as the sixth member. Confederacy members referred to themselves as "Haudenosaunee," The People of the Longhouse. Sawyer, The Six Nations Confederacy.

a feint, only committing a few companies, which were routed piecemeal as they met the British. "This sending of successive small detachments to assail an unknown force in the darkness, instead of concentrating his forces in some good defensive position, shows clearly enough that General Hall had little idea of the proper course to be taken."[174]

The only notable resistance was by Colonel Blakeslie and his Ontario County regiment who effected severe casualties on the British reinforcements as the second wave of boats arrived. Colonel Chapin leading militia from Buffalo also counterattacked, convincing the men from Genesee County to rally with them, but outnumbered over two to one by experienced British regulars, they were all thrown back in confusion. Most of the militiamen then fled Black Rock, while General Hall hurried from Buffalo with 1,000 militia. Because of desertions on the way to Black Rock, when General Hall arrived, barely 600 Americans were available to oppose a force of over 1,200 British and Mohawks.

General Hall called a retreat which quickly became an unorganized stampede. American officers who had been abandoned by their troops, joined the flight. Colonel Chapin raised a white flag and negotiated with the British, stalling them to give the citizens time to flee. The Buffalo militia hurried back to their homes to take care of their families. When they got to Buffalo ahead of the enemy, "They declared that the Americans were whipped, that the British were marching on the town, and most terrible of all that the Indians were coming. Then all was confusion and dismay. Teams were at a premium. Horses, oxen, sleighs, sleds, wagons, carts—nearly everything that had feet, wheels or runners—were pressed into service. Most took care to secure some provisions and bedding, threw them promiscuously

---

[174] Johnson, *Centennial History of Erie County*, 248.

into whatever vehicle they could obtain, and started. Children were half smothered with feather beds, babies alternated with loaves of bread. Many, who neither had nor could obtain teams, set forth on foot. Men, women, and children by the score were seen hastening through the snow and half frozen mud."[175] By the time the British troops arrived, most people had evacuated Buffalo, leaving the town almost empty.

The British burned the village of Black Rock, including three American warships that were part of the victorious fleet under Commodore Perry earlier in the year. The British burned all but three of the two hundred buildings in Buffalo. A total of forty American militia and citizens lost their lives, but ninety were captured and taken to Canada; among those taken prisoner was Dr. William Sheldon. "The [British Mohawks] Indians were let loose upon the flying inhabitants, and hundreds of them were overtaken and massacred. The frontier presented one scene of universal desolation."[176]

Daniel Davis certainly would have been shocked by the disaster, coming so fast after the attack on Fort Niagara and Lewiston. He certainly would have seen the refugees arriving at LeRoy. After collecting several hundred militia fleeing Buffalo, General Hall stopped at Williamsville so his troops could protect the throngs of people fleeing Buffalo. He called for reinforcements in case of further invasion. Likely, Daniel Davis had his LeRoy regiment on alert and marched to Batavia as soon as he heard from General Hall. He must have been disappointed in the New York militia's ineffectiveness at Buffalo, particularly in Major Adams of the Batavian regiment, who had been too sick to fight at Black Rock at the skirmish the previous summer, then made no distinction in the recent attack on Buffalo. To learn from the events, perhaps Daniel encountered one Private

---

[175] Johnson, *Centennial History of Erie County*, 249.
[176] Beers, 34.

Lathrop when he arrived in Batavia to discuss the battle. Abigal Lathrop was at the burning of Buffalo, so it appears he had fought to the end before he retreated.[177] Perhaps Mr. Lathrop told Daniel he had seen his friend Dr. William Sheldon taken prisoner at the skirmish in Black Rock when Major Adams's battalion had retreated. His whereabouts were unknown.[178]

Colonel Daniel Davis's 99th Regiment had not been called to the Niagara Frontier yet, but it certainly appeared that the militiamen of LeRoy would be next. Daniel was likely eager to enter the conflict and make up for the New York militia's mediocre performance. Certainly, he was confident his men would follow him.

---

[177] Beers, 289.
[178] "Sheldon was captured by the British and sent to Montreal where he was severely treated. He was released six months later but carried a deep hatred for the British all his life." Belluscio, June *8, 1812-2012, Our Bicentennial.*

Brigadier General Daniel Davis and the War of 1812

Michael A. Ponzio

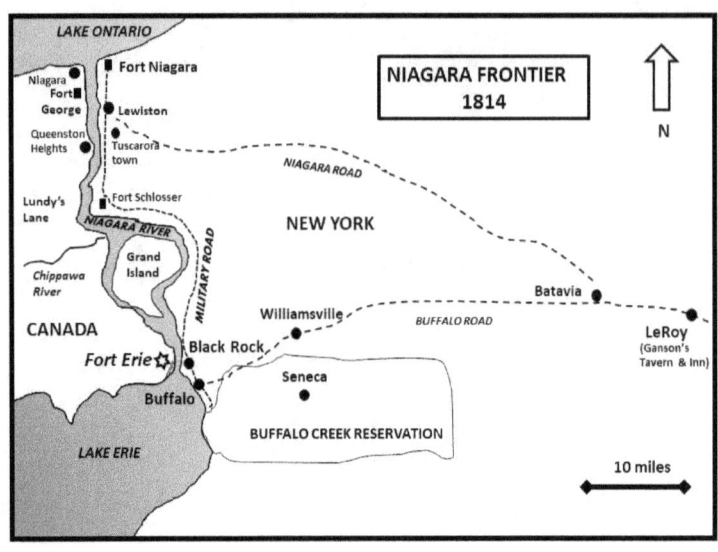

SOURCE:
From the collection of the LeRoy Historical Society.
Director, Lynne Belluscio.

CHAPTER XII: Niagara Frontier, Summer 1814

Major Winfield Scott of the U.S. Army, had earned a reputation in May 1813 for bravery and leadership. He had been among the first to leap from the boats during his brigade's amphibious landing north of Fort George. Leading his men, Major Scott repulsed the bayonet charge by the British infantry and established a beachhead on the shore of Lake Ontario. He broke his collarbone in a fall from his horse during the subsequent battle, but Scott continued to lead his men, seizing Fort George from the British. After the battle, he voiced his dissatisfaction to his superiors, whose orders he claimed had allowed the retreating British to escape, possibly lengthening the war.

Later in 1813, Scott was with the force that failed in their attempt to invade Lower Canada at Montreal. He went to Washington, D.C., to voice his allegations of incompetence by the leading generals, at both Niagara and Montreal. As a result of his blunt honesty, the U.S. Army promoted him to colonel and assigned him to the Niagara Frontier, where he standardized the training of the infantry, drilling the men twelve hours per day under strict discipline.

Colonel Winfield Scott's methods certainly made an impression on his fellow soldiers and his superiors, because in March 1814, the U.S. command promoted him to Brigadier General. Scott was only twenty-seven. About the same time, Governor Tompkins of New York promoted Daniel Davis ahead of the four other regiment commanders in Genesee County as Brigadier General of the 6th Brigade Militia.[179]

Had Daniel been following Scott's progress? Perhaps he identified with Scott's orderly methods and the general's self-confidence. Winfield Scott demanded strict discipline of his men. "The troops idolized him."[180] Similarly, the Genesee Gazette wrote of Daniel Davis, "He was a man greatly beloved by those who served under him, though a strict disciplinarian."[181]

In the summer of 1814, U.S. Army Brigadier General Jacob Brown organized another American invasion of Upper Canada. On the night of July 3, General Scott crossed the Niagara River with a brigade of regulars, followed by another American brigade under General Ripley. Their first goal was to seize British Fort Erie, opposite Black Rock. At the Americans' approach, the small garrison, fewer than 200 defenders, began firing their artillery, but then quickly ceased, surrendering when they discovered that there were 4,500 troops in the attacking force. Brown garrisoned the newly occupied Fort Erie with militia, issuing plans for them to improve the fortifications. He also organized transport across the river to use Buffalo as a supply base. Within a few days, he marched north with the two brigades of regulars and a third brigade commanded by General Porter, his force comprising militia and volunteer Native Americans.

---

[179] The date Brigadier General of the 6th Brigade, Alexander Rea died is unknown, but he was listed as deceased, with Daniel Davis promoted in his place, on the March 2, 1814, *Military Minutes of the Council of Appointment of the State of New York*, 1783-1821, Volume 2.
[180] Barbuto, *The Canadian Theater 1814*, 23.
[181] North, *"Our County and Its People,"* 146.

The latter group was "a party of six hundred Iroquois warriors—Seneca, Oneida, Onondaga, and Tuscarora men, with a few women as well—fighting under the command of the elderly Seneca chief, Red Jacket."[182]

After two days' march north, the American forces encountered the British accompanied by their Iroquois Mohawk allies under General Drummond near Chippawa Creek. At the Battle of Chippawa, the Americans defeated the British regulars, showing that the U.S. Army regulars could match the soldiers of the largest empire in the world.

The British retreated to Fort George, reinforcements arrived from York, and within a few weeks again challenged the invading Americans at the Battle of Lundy's Lane, in which both armies suffered numerous casualties. Severely bloodied and exhausted, both forces fought to a stalemate, with the Americans returning to Fort Erie to resupply.

General Scott's brigade fought exceptionally well, but the casualty rate was very high, including Scott himself, who was severely wounded. Again criticizing his superior officer, "Scott believed that Brown's decision to refrain from fully committing his strength at the outset of this battle resulted in the destruction of Scott's brigade and a high number of unnecessary deaths." [183]

The day after the battle, militiamen rowed the wounded General Scott across the Niagara, then carried him on a litter to Buffalo, then Batavia, because his wounds would not tolerate the jarring motion from wheeled conveyance. At Batavia "he stayed at the comfortable house of his friend Mr. Brisbane, where he was nursed by the kindness of his sister, Mrs. Carey."[184]

The residents of western New York highly respected General Scott for his part in defending the frontier. General Brown sent

---

[182] Ibid., 14.
[183] Berton, *Flames Across the Border, 1813-1814.*, 429.
[184] Scott, *Memoirs of Lieut.-General Winfield Scott*, 80.

a report to Secretary of War Armstrong noting that *"Scott is entitled to the highest honors our country can bestow to him, more than to any other man, am I indebted for the [Chippawa] victory of the fifth of July.* Scott stands out as the person most closely associated with this victory, not only for his inspirational battlefield leadership but also for his work in training his officers and men during the months preceding the invasion."[185] The citizens of Batavia, upon hearing of his heroics, were thrilled to host the general for his recuperation.

In his autobiography, General Scott wrote that by August he was not healing and wanted to be treated by the surgeon, Dr. Physick of Philadelphia.[186] Citizens of Batavia carried him on a mattress by litter to LeRoy, then at each town, the bearers passed on his litter to local volunteers, who conveyed him to the next town, and so forth, until he reached Geneva. Beers states, "He was borne in a litter to the Ganson tavern, where all turned out to do him honor."[187] There are conflicting stories where General Scott completed his recuperation. One source states it was in Batavia, another source says that he stayed several months at Ganson's tavern, but most sources show that Dr. Physick, who practiced in Philadelphia, did treat him. When General Scott was brought through LeRoy, he most likely stayed at least one night, and the best place would have been at the renowned Ganson's Tavern, which had been expanded. "John Ganson, Jr., was its proprietor, and under him the hostelry became one of the most

---

[185] Barbuto, *The Canadian Theater 1814*, 23.

[186] Physick, the "Father of American Surgery", greatly improved the treatment of fractures, invented the stomach pump, introduced catgut sutures to replace silk and flax, and developed instruments for removing tonsils. Among Physick's patients were the daughters of Presidents' John Adams and James Monroe, First Lady Dolly Madison, signer of the Declaration Dr. Benjamin Rush, General Winfield Scott, and Chief Justice John Marshall. *Philip Syng Physick, 1768-1837*

[187] Beers, 475.

noted for the accommodation of the traveler between Albany and the lakes, a reputation which it retained for the whole period it was used as a public house."[188]

If Beers was accurate in stating *"at Ganson tavern, all turned out to do him honor,"* likely Daniel Davis also paid him a visit, along with Dr. William Sheldon, the leading doctor in LeRoy and the military surgeon in Daniel's brigade. Although Daniel was ten years older than General Scott, it's possible he saw him as a mentor. During the general's stay at Ganson's Tavern, certainly he would have asked Scott about British tactics and battle methods.

While he recuperated in Geneva, Scott improved enough to take a carriage to Albany, continued on a steamboat down the Hudson River to New York City, and then went on to Philadelphia where Dr. Physick treated him for several months. The general did not fully recover until after the war.

"Winfield Scott during his career was a U.S. Army general, diplomat, and presidential candidate. Known as 'Grand Old Man of the Army,' he served on active duty as a general longer than any other man in American history and most historians rate him the ablest American commander of his time. Over the course of his fifty-year career, he commanded forces in the War of 1812, the Mexican-American War, the Black Hawk War, the Second Seminole War, and, briefly, the American Civil War, conceiving the Union strategy known as the Anaconda Plan that would be used to defeat the Confederacy."[189]

On August 4, 1814, the British force in Upper Ontario arrived at Fort Erie, which the Americans had decided to defend to keep their foothold in Canada. General Brown, recuperating from a

---

[188] Beers, 455.
[189] "Winfield Scott," *New World Encyclopedia.*

wound at the Battle of Lundy's Lane, had been replaced by General Gaines, who had directed the American forces to improve the fortifications, lengthening Fort Erie's earthen walls of a few hundred yards to a half mile long and constructing several batteries of artillery on raised mounds or platforms. He also had his men fell trees, erecting an abatis, with sharpened branches facing the enemy. Babcock, in his *Siege of Fort Erie*, described the details. "The following improvements were commenced: an earthwork from the southerly side of the fort to the hillock on our extreme left; an embrasure on the hillock for Towson's battery of five guns; two bastions on the west side of the fort; embrasures for Riddle's and Fontaine's batteries; an earthwork running easterly from the fort towards Niagara River, with an embrasure for Douglass's battery on the easterly end; numerous camp traverses; an abatis from the Niagara River on our right, extending clear around the works to the river on our left; and the completion of the redoubt commenced by McDonough. It will be seen that these improvements converted a very weak fort into a rather strong position, and the fort changed into a fortified camp with the rear open and protected by the Niagara."

British General Drummond did not have the supplies for a protracted siege. In addition, his troops were living in crude shacks full of water and mud because of relentless daily rain, degrading troop effectiveness. He decided to assault the fort. Drummond brought long-range cannons from Fort George, bombarding the Americans for several days before launching a nighttime assault on August 13. The British troops breached the walls, resulting in vicious hand-to-hand combat, but the

American defenders repulsed the assault. The British lost over 200 killed in the attack, but there were fewer than 20 American fatalities.

The days after the failed attack, the British guns resumed bombarding Fort Erie, some days firing 500 rounds of artillery, injuring many Americans including the commanding officer, General Gaines. In addition, with concerns that British reinforcements would arrive,[190] plus with Gaines injured, General Brown, although not fully recovered, returned to duty, launching several sorties, trying to destroy the enemy batteries. These limited counterattacks failed, inducing Brown to request Governor Thompkins for additional militia. He also asked militia commander General Amos Hall for help, but he did not receive a significant response until Brigadier General Porter organized recruitment. Then, thousands of New York militiamen volunteered. Would it be Daniel Davis's turn to serve?

During the first week Fort Erie was under siege, peace negotiations between the United States and Great Britain began in Ghent, Belgium. An impasse occurred when the Americans would not accept Great Britain's demand to establish an independent Native American state as a buffer between the United States and Canada. (The proposed land for the nation would have been present day Ohio and Michigan—U.S. territories).

The peace talks ensued, and on August 24, the British landed an army on the shores of Chesapeake Bay, easily defeated the

---

[190] On September 7, a British courier was captured revealing that two more regiments were enroute to reinforce General Drummond. Whitehorne, *The Battle for Fort Erie*, 84.

U.S. forces, and burned Washington, D.C. Other startling news followed. Britain's war with Napoleon had ended, allowing the transfer of 16,000 veteran British troops to North America, after which there began a series of coordinated offensives intending to occupy American territory before the end of the negotiations.

The U.S. Army and militias would see their greatest challenge of the war on multiple fronts. Two days after they burned the U.S. capital, the British invaded Maine. They easily chased out the few American defenders and declared it part of Canada, the province of New Ireland. Before the end of August, the largest army amassed for a single battle in the war, 11,000 British soldiers, invaded northern New York, marching along Lake Champlain.

Some British veterans from the Napoleonic wars were in the army besieging Fort Erie. If the British seized the fort, would they continue across the Niagara and repeat the devastation they had imparted along the Niagara Frontier the previous year, and continue to LeRoy?

These events and the nearby siege of Fort Erie alarmed Daniel Davis. Just weeks before, the British had conducted a massive assault on the Americans at Fort Erie. The enemy had penetrated the walls, captured one of the batteries inside the fort, and turned the guns around to fire at the Americans. Above the din of battle, "British Colonel Drummond shouted orders for his infantry, armed with bayonets, *'to give the damned Yankee rascals no quarter!'*"[191] The fort was close to falling when the captured battery magazine exploded, killing a hundred British instantly, but few Americans. The assault was repulsed, but the Americans desperately needed reinforcements.

Certainly, among all the dangers, Daniel Davis was determined to ensure his family was safe. His reaction was

---

[191] *The War of 1812 - Siege of Fort Erie.*

decisive and forthright, as described in a letter to Governor Thompkins from John Yates, an attorney commissioned as an officer by the governor. Part of this letter is transcribed below.

> *"J. B. Yates to Governor D. D. Tompkins. Buffalo, September 3, 1814.*
> *Dear Sir,*
> *The militia are collecting at this place very rapidly. There is every probability that more will turn out than were required by the order. Everything has been done to rouse the feelings of the community, and the exertions for that purpose have apparently been attended with very great success.*
> *Brigadier General Davis of Genesee County has ordered out his whole brigade without any requisition or authority. Yet, as it was considered that they might be usefully employed, it was thought proper not to discourage him. If he were regularly ordered out, he would take the command from General Porter. This would by no means answer in the present situation of things, as it would occasion very general dissatisfaction."*[192]

Because Daniel Davis had ordered out his whole brigade, he would have outranked General Porter, who had been successfully leading the militia *from the front*, through the bloodiest battles of the war. After all that General Porter and his men had been through together, had he been replaced, the morale of the troops could have been affected. Accordingly, the governor promoted Porter to Brevet Major General, from a one-star general to a two-star general, so he would outrank Brigadier Daniel Davis. Before the governor had announced Porter's

---

[192] Cruikshank, *The Documentary History of the Campaign on the Niagara Frontier in 1814*, 192.

promotion, Daniel Davis had already willingly committed to serve under General Porter.

In a remarkable manner, Daniel Davis answered the call and marched his men to Williamsville, several miles from Black Rock, although his 6th brigade was not directly ordered to assemble. To gather five regiments together in a short time showed the loyalty and respect his men had for him. The author of the referenced letter, Lt. Colonel J.B. Yates, was an aide to Governor Thompson sent to Buffalo to assist in gathering the militia. Well aware of the previous problems recruiting the militia, as well as some militia units that had refused to cross into Canada, Yates likely recommended the US Army should not reject the Genesee Brigade and dampen their volunteer spirit.

Cruikshank writes, "There could no longer be room to doubt that the New York Militia were assembling in great numbers. Brigadier Daniel Davis of Genesee County had ordered his entire brigade into service without authority, and it had been accepted. The force upon the march was actually reported to be considerably in excess of the number required and was estimated at between 4000 and 5000 men. Confident in their numbers they were said to be in excellent spirits and perfectly willing to cross the river, but many of them were poorly armed and equipped."[193]

The official document from President Madison for the New York Militia to muster stated, "Every soldier must furnish himself with a musket or rifle, knapsack, canteen, cartridge box, three flints, a watch coat, and clothing for three months. Those who are unable to equip themselves with muskets and rifles or cartridge boxes will be supplied from the public deposit, but it is required by the Commander-in-Chief that all who can supply themselves should do so."[194]

---

[193] Cruikshank, *The Siege of Fort Erie, August 1st-September 23rd, 1814*, 32.
[194] Cruikshank, *The Documentary History of the Campaign on the Niagara Frontier in 1814*, 438.

The state armory was in Onondaga County, and the closest arsenal to LeRoy was in Batavia. Turner described the patriotism of a physician in the village of Bergen, who besides practicing medicine, served as supervisor of the village and as a deacon of the First Congregational Church. "In an exigency of anticipated invasion, and a want of arms, Dr. Ward collected all the muskets, rifles, cartouch boxes and bayonets in his neighborhood, and delivered them to Colonel Daniel Davis for the use of his Regiment [sic]. Twenty-one muskets, and cartouch boxes, and bayonets, and four rifles, and besides all the powder and balls of the new settlement were put in requisition."[195] Beers added that Ward "was evidently a good deal of a man."[196]

---

[195] Turner, *History of the Pioneer Settlement*, 556.
[196] Beers, 355.

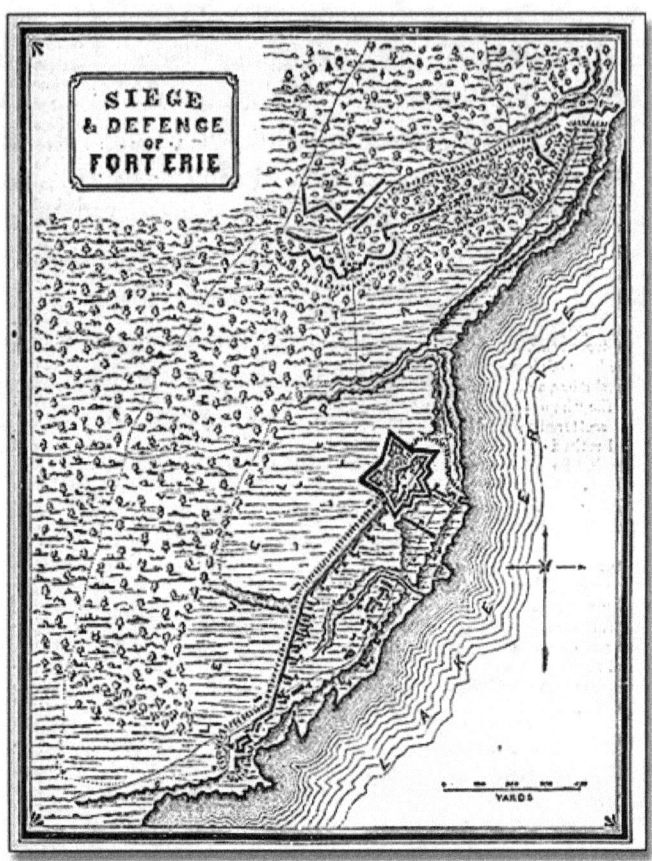

Source: Lossing, Benson J., The Pictoral Field Book of the War of 1812. This work is in the public domain because its copyright had expired in the United States and those countries with copyright term of no more than the life of the author plus 100 years. https:wikicommons.org Old Fort Erie Lossing

CHAPTER XIII: Muster of the 6th Brigade

In late August 1814, Major General Porter published a fervent appeal to the militia of the western counties of New York. Daniel Davis, as brigadier general of the Genesee County militia, may have been mailed a copy of the bulletin. Most likely, it was printed in the Batavian *Advocate*.

General Porter wrote, referring to the defense by the American troops at the siege of Fort Erie:

"If the fate of the gallant little [American] army which for six weeks past has been wading through fields of blood for your security, composed in part, too, of your own immediate neighbors and friends, cannot move you to action, I admonish you to recollect that on the support, and the immediate and vigorous support, of that army depends your own security. That [American] army destroyed and your fruitful fields, your stately edifices and your fair possessions are laid waste. Your women and children will feel the weight of the tomahawk. Nay, even liberty itself, without which those blessings are of no estimation in a patriot's heart, will forsake a country so unworthy of her protection. During the assault upon Fort Erie the British commander had 400 savages in sight of our

Michael A. Ponzio

intrenchments, [sic] ready to leap in should the scales of victory incline to his side and complete the work of destruction, and this same scourge will follow him through the country the moment that the [U.S.] army, its only barrier, shall be broken down. Should the enemy succeed there is nothing on this side [of] Utica can resist his force or escape his ravages."[197]

By September 1, 1814, most of the able-bodied men in LeRoy had left for Williamsville, a week or two before the usual start of the harvest. Daniel Davis's older children would have to bear the task of caring for the homestead. He could be absent for the entire three-month term. Naomi, at 14, would have been an immense help to her mother, Naomi Le Barron Davis, who possibly was still pregnant with her seventh child, who would be born later that year. Their oldest sons, Alfred, 13, and Asher, 11, might try to get the next two younger children, Cynthia, nine, and David, seven, to help with the work. Leveritt, only five, would stay close to the house doing chores.

Across the road, James Davis Jr. was 39 years old, still within the range (age 18 to 45) required under law to serve in the militia, but no records show when he was in the militia nor what rank. If he marched to war, his oldest sons, Lewis, 14, and Eden, 10, would have to bring in the harvest. James's wife, Jehannah Wilcocks Davis, would supervise their youngest, six year old Ezra, working in the garden.

A half mile east of James's farm lived Norton S. Davis, the youngest brother of Daniel and James. Norton was a lieutenant in the 77th Regiment of Daniel's brigade.[198] He was married and

---

[197] Cruikshank, *The Documentary History of the Campaign on the Niagara Frontier in 1814*, 27.
[198] *Military Minutes of the Council of Appointment: 1783-1821*, 1248.

their first child had not yet been born, so his nephews down the road would likely help on his farm when he left for Buffalo.

Local citizens that were exempt from the militia included those involved in the federal postal system, such as post masters, stagecoach drivers, and ferrymen that served postal routes. Marine captains and their crew who were employed within the United States and men over forty-five were also exempted. "They would be available to help in the harvest, and most likely were snagged by the industrious women organizing planting and harvesting 'bees' while the younger men were gone."[199]

The older men were organized into a militia company by Dr. Ward, the energetic man who had collected weapons for General Davis. The group comprised those too old to fight, and instead protected the home front. Dr. Ward was elected as captain of the troop of exempts, or "silver grays."[200] The roster included a drummer and a fifer.

After an overnight bivouac in Williamsville, the host of 4,000 militia progressed to Buffalo. The numbers were greater than expected, and the U.S. command was scrambling to get enough food and supplies for the volunteers. It appeared, however, that enough weapons would be available, as stated by Colonel Yates in his letter to the governor, "I have also written to Mr. Hopper at Onondaga [the state armory]. The arms at Canandaigua and Batavia have been taken for the use of the detachment. Men have been sent out to collect such as may be in the hands of individuals and have not been returned. These, together with such United States arms as can be procured and British arms

---

[199] Beers, 591.
[200] Turner, O., *History of the Pioneer Settlement*, 557.

taken from the enemy, will probably be sufficient to arm the men." [201]

The rank and file were armed, but what about the officers? The 1792 Militia Act passed by Congress stated, "Each commissioned officer shall be armed with a sword or hanger [short hunting sword] and spontoon [officer's lance]."[202] Daniel Davis was armed with a sword that under the law of 1792 he was obliged to furnish at his own expense. His battle sword would eventually be passed down through generations of Davises.[203]

By the time the army of militiamen had arrived in Buffalo, about September 5, their count was closer to 3,000. Much of Buffalo had been rebuilt, so the merchants had returned, but even with government stores, the town strained to feed the large number of men. Either the initial estimate was high or possibly some might have returned to their farms. Perhaps the patriotic emotions that had been instilled by Porter's eloquent plea for recruits and Davis's charismatic summons of the entire 6th brigade had cooled. The deserters, those that may have changed their mind about volunteering, could have been penalized. "Over the course of the war, 4,000 militiamen were fined for refusing to show up for service."[204]

---

[201] Cruikshank, *Documentary History of the Campaign on the Niagara Frontier in 1814*, 192.

[202] A spontoon was a spear weapon resembling a halberd, last used by officers in the Napoleonic Wars. Lewis and Clark, American explorers of the Louisiana Purchase each carried one in 1804. Esch, *Our Second Line: The National Guard*, 19.

[203] See Chapter XVII: *The Destiny of the two Swords*.

[204] Historians of the War of 1812 have not emphasized the anti-war sentiment in New York and how it affected the performance of the militia during the war; instead, they stressed the anti-war sentiment in New England. The response of New York's militia, for example, at the battle of Queenston, reflected, in part, the deep divisions the war created in New York and the politicization of the state's militia. Strum, *New York Militia and Opposition to the War of 1812*, 114.

Brigadier General Daniel Davis and the War of 1812

There were also women in the fighting ranks—Native American women. "The Onondagas in central New York, had allied with the United States since the federal Treaty of Canandaigua of 1794, joining the Americans against the British. The most famous of the women fighters was Dinah John, an Onondaga, whose husband Thomas John, fought at the battles of Chippawa, Lundy's Lane, and Fort Erie. Dinah accompanied him for a part of his enlistment time."205

The year before, six hundred Iroquois warriors had fought on the American side at the Battle of Chippawa; Mohawks, fighting for the British, faced Senecas, Onondagas, and Tuscaroras, allied with the Americans. There were eighty Iroquois fatalities during a fierce skirmish between the opposing bands. Shocked after killing their former allies, some of whom were in the same clan, the Iroquois tribes of New York officially withdrew from the war. Individuals were still free to fight as volunteers. Those who remained to fight included fewer than fifty Iroquois, led by Red Jacket, who stayed with the American army and fought in the Battle of Fort Erie.

Brigadier General Davis likely had his men set up temporary camp at Buffalo because generals Brown and Porter planned to send the militia across the river to Fort Erie within four or five days. They were waiting until a flotilla of forty scows was built. The large flat-bottomed boats with sloping, square ends were being constructed for the purpose of transporting the men across the river.206 Aaron Tufts, a soldier in Daniel's brigade, observed, "After the arrival of [General] Davis at camp in Buffalo, things went quiet and orderly."207 Although no shoes or uniforms were issued to the militia, they were promised tents when they got to Fort Erie, especially helpful, because it had

---

[205] Hauptman, *They Also Served: American Indian Women in the War of 1812*.
[206] Cruikshank, *The Siege of Fort Erie*, 32.
[207] Samson, *History of Brigadier Daniel Davis*.

been raining almost every day. In contrast, the British troops besieging the fort were without tents and were miserable in their lean-to sheds covered with tree branches against the adverse weather.

General Davis's close friend and aide-de-camp, Dr. William Sheldon, was among the general's staff in Buffalo. Also present was Daniel's neighbor, Major Benjamin Ganson, the youngest son of the late John Ganson. Another neighbor, Captain Asa Buel, was leading a company. Both officers were with the 77th New York state militia regiment. Daniel's youngest brother, Norton S. Davis, a lieutenant in the 77th, was probably there. Other staff members of the 6th brigade at the camp reporting to Brigadier General Davis were Colonel Worth Churchill, the commandant of the 164th Regiment, and two of his battalion commanders, Major S. Kellogg and Major Shaball Dunham. Major Simon Pierson of Fort Hill may have also been present.

A Seneca volunteer, William Parker, from Genesee County, may have traveled to Buffalo with the 6th brigade.[208] Perhaps he camped with his Iroquois countrymen, Native American volunteers from the Seneca or Tuscarora reservations.

Most of the troops waiting to cross the Niagara River were militia from western New York, joining others from ten states. They had come from as far away as Tennessee and Vermont. Also, there was a company fighting for the United States made up of pro-U.S. Canadians as well as Americans who had moved to Upper Canada. Their leader, Joseph Wilcocks, had been killed a few days earlier during a sortie against one of the British batteries that had been pounding the Americans inside Fort Erie. The unsuccessful attack had not silenced any of the enemy's long guns, confirming the need to call out the additional militias.

---

[208] Beers, 122.

By now the American buildup was obvious to the British. Ironically, the enemy spies in Buffalo had only to read the Buffalo Gazette of August 30, 1814, to learn that numerous militias were gathering near the village. The newspaper reported more troops were arriving daily.[209]

On September 8, Major General Porter met with the militia officers. Porter reminded his staff of the problem at the Battle of Queenston Heights two years earlier, when the bulk of the militia refused to cross into Canada. Certainly, General Davis was present at the meeting, recalling the event with disdain. Porter made clear to the officers that he did not want the catastrophe of Queenston repeated.

The next morning on a chilly and misty day in Buffalo, General Porter addressed the assembled militia, encouraging them to bravery, to fight for their families, their country, and their comrades suffering in Fort Erie. "A few hundred volunteered immediately." One would assume Daniel certainly came forward right away, his brother Norton, Dr. Sheldon, and others from his brigade with him. "Then as a band played martial music, Porter marched these men around the others. Heartened by the opportunity to fight under Generals Brown and Porter to break the siege at Fort Erie, hundreds more joined them."[210] Eventually, half of the 3,000 militiamen volunteered to cross the Niagara River.

The volunteers broke camp and formed their companies, ready to march to Black Rock to cross over to Fort Erie. "When the command to move off was given a militiaman stepped out of the ranks and shouted out, 'We are militia of New York and cannot be ordered out of the state. It is unconstitutional.'"[211] Strum explains, "Under the New York state constitution, the

---

[209] Cruikshank, *The Siege of Fort Erie*, 32.
[210] Barbuto, The *Canadian Theater 1814*, 39.
[211] Babcock, *The Siege of Fort Erie: An Episode of the War of 1812*, 53.

militia was a defensive force, and militiamen did not have to participate in offensive operations requiring an invasion of Canada. Men serving in the militia expected to protect their families, their communities, and New York, and did not expect to invade Canada. Throughout the war Federalists hammered away at this point, and repeatedly discouraged militiamen, Federalists and Republicans, from engaging in offensive operations."[212]

A ruckus started, but General Porter ordered a squad of regulars to seize the agitator. Most likely General Davis and his officers helped quell the emotions. Calm was restored. The outspoken man was taken to Williamsville and told if he returned to Buffalo, he would be shot.

The militiamen who had agreed to cross into Upper Canada trudged for two hours through the rain to Black Rock. "None of the New York militiamen were in uniform, so General Porter ordered them to wear red cloths round their necks or heads to show they were members of his brigade."[213] To help conceal the size of their force, on the night of September 9, about 1,000 of the militia crossed to Fort Erie aboard the fleet of scows. Three American schooners that had arrived from Erie, Pennsylvania, with more troops escorted the crossing. The next day on September 10, the rest of the militiamen were ferried to Fort Erie. They joined the other militia at the south end of the fortifications next to Snake Hill where Towson's Battery of artillery was located. They were billeted in tents with board floors, protected by sod and log breastworks.

About the time the second group of militiamen arrived and were drying out in their tents, eating, and resting, General Brown, the commander of the combined forces at Fort Erie, called a council of war with his top officers. Certainly, General

---

[212] Strum, "New *York Militia and Opposition to the War of 1812*", 115.
[213] Whitehorne, *While Wahington Burned: The Battle for Fort Erie*, 77.

Davis would be attending. Daniel had heard rumors that Brown wanted to attack the British right away.

GENESEE COUNTY MILITIA COMMANDING OFFICERS 1814

7TH Division- Major General Amos Hall (Bloomfield, Ontario County)
6th Brigade- Brigadier General Daniel Davis (Le Roy)
31st Regiment- Lt. Colonel John Acheson (Parma)
77th Regiment- Lt. Colonel Jedediah Crosby (Le Roy)
99th Regiment- Lt. Colonel William Vary (Sheldon)
161st Regiment- Lt. Colonel Mattias Lemen (Williamsburg)
164th Regiment- Lt. Colonel Worth L. Churchill (Bennington)

Source: Military minutes of the council of appointment of the state of New York, 1783-1821. V. 2 (familysearch.org)

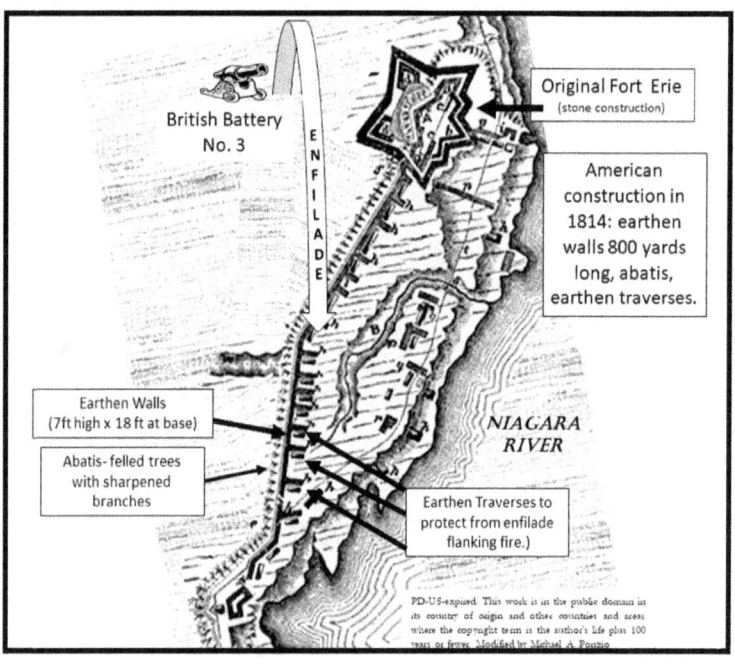

CHAPTER XIV: The Militia Prepares

Major General Jacob Brown, the commander-in-chief of the American forces on the Niagara Frontier, led the war council. Attendees included senior officers such as the regimental colonels and the brigadier generals. Likely present at the council were Brigadier General Miller, head of the U.S. Army 1st Brigade; Brigadier General Ripley, commanding the U.S. Army 2nd Brigade; and Brevet Major General Porter of the NY State Militia, leading the volunteers. Militia Brigadier General Daniel Davis reported directly to Porter and certainly would have been present. Davis's subordinates that might have attended were Colonel Crosby, who took over the NY State Militia 77th Regiment when Daniel was promoted to general, as well as Colonel Worth Churchill, commander of the 164th Regiment. Both officers were from Genesee County. Historical records show both colonels fought alongside Daniel at Fort Erie.

At this meeting, held on the evening of September 10, General Brown advocated a sortie for the morning of the 11th against the British batteries before the enemy learned details of the American reinforcements. The primary target was battery No. 3, (three twenty-four-pounders, an eight-inch howitzer, and a mortar) only 400 yards distant, which had been pounding the American camps for a week. Its position on the west end of the British siege fortifications allowed the cannons to enfilade[214] the American defenses. Deserters reported to Brown that the British had three brigades, leaving one on their front line at the trenches and batteries, while the other two rested in the British camp two miles north. One of Brown's brigade commanders, General Ripley, voiced his disagreement with the sortie, arguing it would fail. Most of the officers also opposed the plan, and General Brown delayed the sortie. Later historical sources show that deserters had reported 2,500 American troops had crossed the night of September 10, so as the Americans discussed the assault, the British commanders were clued that a counterattack might happen.

Because of Daniel Davis's eagerness to help his comrades-in-arms at Fort Erie, it's likely he would have agreed with General Brown to attack. Was General Ripley's opposition because of an earlier conflict with General Brown? A month before, at the Battle of Lundy's Lane, Brown had accused Ripley of losing the battle when he allowed the British to recover an artillery battery. Ripley had to endure a court martial imposed by Brown to prove he was not incompetent.

Early in the siege of Fort Erie, the Americans had three armed schooners anchored offshore of the fort, which bombarded the enemy entrenchments. A British night attack, however, had overwhelmed the crews and seized two of the boats, the third escaping by sailing into Lake Erie. By September 10, the Americans had reestablished control of the Niagara River after

---

[214] Gunfire directed from a flanking position along the length of an enemy battle line. Enfilade, *Mirriam-Webster Dictionary.*

the arrival of a brig and three armed schooners from Presque Isle at Erie, Pennsylvania. Thus, American supplies and reinforcements could easily cross to Fort Erie. At the opposite end of the Niagara River at Lake Ontario, the American fleet out of Sackett's Harbor, New York, blockaded access to Fort George, preventing the British from sending reinforcements across Lake Ontario. Instead, the British had to use a slower route, marching troops around the western end of the lake.

With these conditions favoring the Americans, General Brown decided the time was right and continued to develop a plan to attack the British held batteries. He arranged for the delivery of hundreds of broadaxes to Fort Erie via Black Rock. On the 15th and 16th, the general ordered bombardment of the British entrenchments. U.S. Army Lieutenants Frazer and Riddle directed militiamen, working in the rain, to remove underbrush and slash two roads through the thick forest, leading from the militia camp at Snake Hill to within 150 yards of Battery No. 3. The trails were blazed in a tortuous path, paralleled each other about thirty yards apart, winding back and forth around the marshy areas created by two weeks of rain. The American sortie could then cover the half mile distance to the British lines concealed by the forest. The British did not detect the American trailblazers, who were hidden by the thick woods, the noise of their activity masked by the American artillery and occasional downpours.

The militiamen had finished clearing the path for the impending sortie. Typically, the militia were assigned more of the labor versus the regular U.S. Army in the camps. They had dug trenches, built up earthen walls seven feet high and eighteen feet thick, created abatis by felling trees and sharpening the branches. And the pioneer farmers may have been more experienced with an axe, having routinely cleared their own land. Daniel Davis probably wasn't involved in creating the assault routes, but some of his men, being hard working, pioneer stock, may have been in the work crews. Beers records several militia privates from LeRoy that fought in the war: Mr. Wilcox, Abraham Buckley, and Joshua Kirkham. Another Genesee militiaman who might have wielded an ax to clear the paths was "Henry Salisbury, who was stationed at Fort Erie."[215] And there was "Amos Spring, who was three times called out in the War of 1812, under Captain Buell and General Davis."[216]

Was General Davis included in formulating the sortie plans, while the work crews cleared the paths? "General Brown worked on his plan in consultation with a few trusted officers but did not reveal the full scheme until late evening of the 16th of September."[217] The plan was for a two-pronged attack to destroy batteries No. 2 and No. 3. A screening force of U.S. Army Rifles and Iroquois, led by Colonel Gibson, would precede two columns under General Porter. Brigadier General Daniel Davis would lead one column and the second column was to be led by U.S. Army Lt. Colonel Wood. A force led by General Miller would be in reserve. Certainly, General Davis was in this group of "trusted officers" because he was leading one of the main assault groups. Whitehorne, in his *Battle for Fort Erie*, refers to Davis's column: "Porter's other column consisted of the Hopkins, Churchill, and Crosby New York regiments, under the command of newly appointed Brigadier General Daniel Davis, an Ontario [sic] [Genesee] farmer, and experienced militia officer."[218]

---

[215] Beers, 289.
[216] Ibid., 552.
[217] Whitehorne, *The Battle for Fort Erie*, 78.
[218] Whitehorne, 79. Genesee County was carved from Ontario County in 1803. Hopkins (Brig Gen Niagara County),

Brigadier General Daniel Davis and the War of 1812

When General Davis returned to his camp after the meeting, he would have briefed his officers on the plans. He may have also learned of the status of the British force that had invaded northern New York. They had reached Plattsburgh. But, in the ensuing battle, the U.S. naval squadron had defeated the British gunboats on Lake Champlain, severing their supply lines and forcing the invading army to retreat to Canada. Daniel likely directed his officers not to reveal the good news to their men yet because a general announcement would be made the next morning to give them heart before the sortie. Also, because of the slow communications, the U.S. forces at Fort Erie did not realize that the previous day, the British had failed to take Fort McHenry and Baltimore after a daylong bombardment.

What if General Brown's plan didn't succeed in breaking the siege? Would the British retake Fort Erie, invade western New York, and repeat the devastation of the previous year? The Americans had repulsed the British invasions in northern New York and Baltimore. It was now the New Yorkers' turn to defend their country.

Lt. Col. Worth Churchill 164th regiment-Genesee County, and Lt. Col. Jedediah Crosby 77th regiment-Genesee County.

Michael A. Ponzio

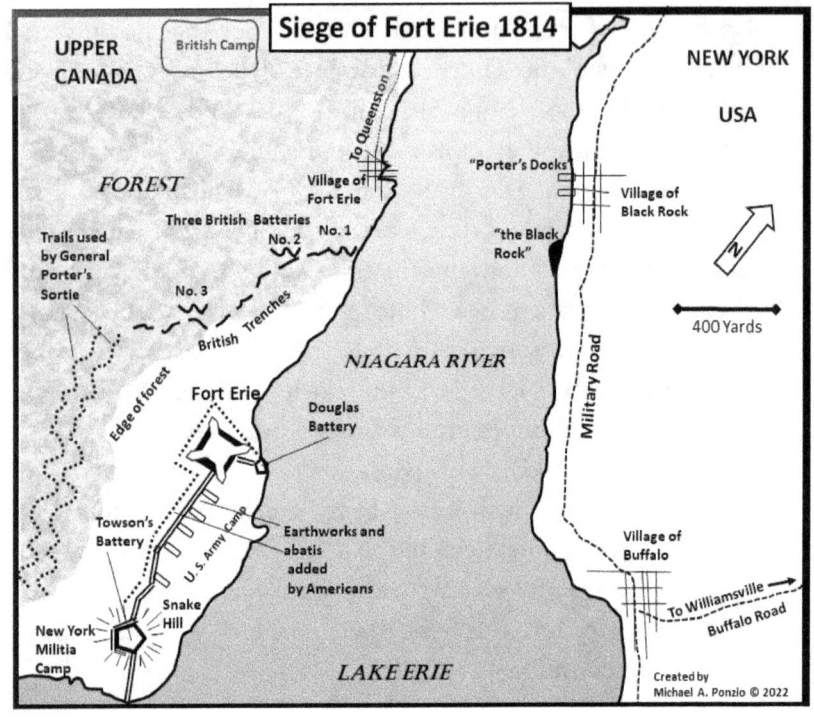

CHAPTER XV: The Sortie from Fort Erie

The weather at Fort Erie on Saturday morning, September 17, 1814, was the same as it had been for the last two weeks: chilly and rainy. A fog hung above the clear-cut, treeless plain in front of the fortifications, obscuring the dense forest the men would slog through by noon. The morale of the American troops was good as they woke in their tents, provided with wooden floors, relatively dry, gathering around the campfire to chase away the chill, eating their usual rations of salted pork and biscuits. The lieutenants (perhaps Lt. Norton S. Davis among them) and captains were going from campfire to campfire, notifying the men of their role in the sortie against the British batteries. The officers also spread the news from the northern front. "A handbill was read, announcing the glorious victories won on Lake Champlain and at Plattsburg a few days before. The news was joyfully received, and the sortie enthusiastically welcomed."[219] When the volunteer militia had gathered to cross the Niagara River to Fort Erie a week earlier on September 10, General Porter had required them to wear a red bandana around

---

[219] Johnson, Crisfield, *Centennial history of Erie County, New York*, 286.

their neck or on their head, since they did not wear uniforms. Many had not kept their red strips of cloth or had lost their bandanas, so as the officers made their rounds to the campfires, "each volunteer was thereupon directed to take off his headgear and tie a red handkerchief or red cloth around his head so that he might be readily distinguished."[220]

How was General Daniel Davis preparing for the assault? His sword most likely would be his only weapon. He probably would not have a pistol. They were expensive and usually only issued to regular army cavalry. Daniel always led from the front to ensure his men were in the right formation that would give them a chance to survive and do their duty. He would have to fight with his sword.

General Daniel Davis's sword was a saber with a curved blade, meant to be wielded with one hand, and had a single cutting edge. The white handle, made of bone, was striated and textured to improve the grip, and was protected by a brass loop guard. The steel blade, decorated thinly with floral wreaths, a cannon, and lightning bolt of gold leaf, had a wide fuller.[221] Daniel possessed a steel officer's sword and although it had decorations, it was functional. In contrast, the standard issue for the American Cavalry, the Starr Sword, was made of iron with a wooden handle and was without decoration.[222] Did Daniel know who made his sword? Unfortunately, the craftsman had not inscribed his name on the blade, a common practice. Daniel's

---

[220] Ibid., 286.
[221] Fuller: a channel in a sword blade, often called "a blood groove", although its purpose has nothing to do with blood. A fuller is used to lighten the blade, much the way that the shape of an I-beam allows a given amount of strength to be achieved with less material, *Groove swords*, Vintage.
[222] The leading sword maker in America from 1798 to 1830 was Connecticut's Nathan Starr. The firm produced a hefty cavalry saber, a no-nonsense enlisted man's edged weapon. 5,000 such pieces were made under the Starr contract of 1812-1813. Worthington, *Nathan Starr 1812 Contract Calvary Saber*.

sword was probably of French origin. Its design matches the same used by high-ranking French officers.[223]

Daniel probably ate breakfast with Colonels Crosby, Churchill, and Hopkins, the commanders of the three regiments in his column, to discuss last-minute details. He had come a long way from his youth in Killingworth, breakfasting on hasty pudding, a corn mush porridge, and hunting passenger pigeons. Certainly, he was determined to protect his family, his community, his country.

Unknown to Daniel, the soldiers defending Battery No. 3 manning the British trenches, the Americans' primary target, were mercenaries of the De Watteville Regiment, an international collection of soldiers. These veteran soldiers had earned distinction in battles of the Napoleonic Wars.[224]

Just before noon, in the relentless fog and light rain, General Brown sent Colonel Gibson with 200 U.S. Army riflemen and about 50 Iroquois as the advance force toward Battery No. 3. He divided General Porter's brigade into two columns. Lieutenant Colonel Wood led the right column, made up of 400 infantrymen from the U.S. Army 23rd Regiment and 500 militia. General Brown had assigned this column to storm the batteries on the British right. Brigadier General Davis was in command of the second column moving along the left trail, parallel to Wood's troops. He was to assist Wood in the attack and oppose the enemy reinforcements when they arrived. Davis's column was made up of three militia regiments. Two were from Genesee

---

[223] Researched using identifying software and online database at https://oldswords.com

[224] General L. De Watteville commanded the Swiss regiment of mercenaries originating from mostly Poland, Lithuania, Germany, Italy, and France. The force fought for Britain in the Napoleonic Wars and at the siege of Fort Erie. Retired veterans were given land in Canada. Perry, *The War of 1812: European Traces in a British-American Conflict.*

County, the 77th led by Lt. Colonel Crosby and the 164th led by Lt. Colonel Churchill. Lt. Colonel Hopkins commanded the third militia regiment. The officers who supervised the ax men who had cleared the paths, lieutenants Frazier and Riddle, guided the columns along the trails. Generals Porter and Brown marched with Davis's column.

At the same time that Porter's columns set out in the forest for No. 3 battery, Brigadier General Miller led a force of regulars out of Fort Erie and hid in a ravine a hundred yards from the British center. They would wait for Porter's attack before assaulting Battery No.2. A reserve force just outside Fort Erie stood by; this force was commanded by General Ripley.

To distract the British and conceal the sound of their approach, the American artillery had begun a heavy bombardment of the enemy lines. The rain became heavier as the two columns in Porter's brigade advanced. The trails had been blazed following a tortuous route, expediently avoiding the low areas that collected water which would become quagmires. Thus, it took over two hours for the American troops to cover the half mile distance to reach a position near the British lines.

The American columns halted several minutes after two o'clock, still undetected in the thick forest with the rain masking their presence, just off the right flank of the British trenches. They were in position to go around the end of the enemy fortifications. As the men waited, at 2:30 p.m., General Brown gave command of the assault force to Porter with the order to attack, and with a few escorts, rushed to join General Miller and his regiment of U.S. Army regulars waiting in the ravine opposite the center of the British lines.

Babcock states that just before they attacked Battery No. 3, the Americans were "a few yards to the right of the enemy's position,"²²⁵ agreeing with Johnson who wrote "Porter's command arrived at the end of the track, within a few rods of Battery No. Three, entirely unsuspected by its occupants."²²⁶

Did the attack begin in the continued silence the Americans had maintained during their approach? Barbuto stated, "Porter's men appeared out of a light fog, surprising the British at Battery Three."²²⁷ Every source agrees the Americans took the defenders of Battery No. 3 completely by surprise, but historian Crisfield Johnson wrote in 1876 that the Americans shouted out as they attacked, "with a tremendous cheer, which was distinctly heard across the river, the men rushed forward."²²⁸ The cheering perhaps sounds very gallant, as if it was the author's embellishment, however, it likely occurred, because Johnson's sources were firsthand witnesses, 'grandfathers' who were alive when the Battle of Fort Erie took place.

The columns of Lt. Colonel Wood and General Davis burst upon the British mercenaries of De Watteville's Regiment, fighting was brief, and the Americans quickly routed the defenders, taking many as prisoners. The Americans took control of the reviled Battery No. 3, spiking the cannons by hammering metal rods into the touch holes. The American attackers also reached a nearby blockhouse which served as a magazine for the battery. The defenders put up a stiff fight, but within a half hour, they were flushed out, and the Americans destroyed the magazine by detonating the stored gunpowder.

Hearing the attack on Battery No. 3, Miller's regulars, hidden in the ravine, headed toward Battery No. 2. "Some militiamen from Porter's brigade escorted the numerous prisoners [over

---

²²⁵ Babcock, 57.
²²⁶ Johnson, 287.
²²⁷ Barbuto, 158.
²²⁸ Johnson, 287.

150] to the rear. The rest, with Porter in the lead, found Miller's column. The two groups pressed on toward the second battery."[229]

Those militiamen in charge of the prisoners might have been Genesee volunteers, but General Davis certainly led most of his column to assist Wood, as well as carry out his primary duty, to face the British reinforcements, as described by Johnson: "Leaving a detachment to spike and dismount the captured cannon, both of Porter's columns dashed forward toward [Battery No. 2] the same object, Gen. Davis leading his volunteers and cooperating closely with Wood."[230]

As the three American forces converged on Battery No. 2, the defenders, having been alerted by the fighting and explosions at Battery No. 3, had prepared for the assault. Also, 2,000 British reinforcements were already on the way from their camp.

At Battery No. 3, the destruction of the gun works continued, the Americans likely used readily available means, hefting cannon balls, smashing the trunnions off the barrels and breaking apart the gun carriages. General Miller's forces arrived at Battery No. 2 about the same time as Porter's two columns, led by Wood and Davis. Most of the gunfire was from the British side because many of the militia's muskets were wet from exposure on the long hike through the woods. "The Americans were received [at Battery No. 2] with a heavy fire, but the three commands combined and carried the battery at the point of the bayonet."[231] Fighting was fierce, but the U.S. forces, by sheer numbers, overwhelmed the defenders, began spiking the cannons, and continued to move east toward Battery No. 1.

As the Americans had surprised the defenders at Battery No. 3, the British reinforcements arrived and counterattacked from

---

[229] Barbuto, *The Canadian Theater*, 40.
[230] Johnson, 287.
[231] Johnson, 287.

the concealment of the surrounding forest. "The falling rain and intervening woods screened them [the British] until at close quarters, when they plied the bayonet with deadly effect upon the disorderly crowd of [Americans] fugitives, whose arms had been generally rendered unserviceable by the rain."[232] As these "first of the British relief forces [Royal Scots and Glengarry Regiment] crashed into the Americans, the New York militia did not hang back but pressed forward. The rain had rendered many muskets inoperative, and much of the fighting was hand to hand."[233] Furthermore, "By all accounts, the New Yorkers fought admirably."[234]

Generals Davis and Wood battled at the front of their men. Wood's regulars had bayonets, but many of Davis's men did not and used their muskets as clubs. The battle had become a jumble of isolated groups in the forest, militia and regulars mixed together, their officers trying to reorganize them. Some of the Americans, hard pressed, retreated as General Ripley brought up the reserves.

Davis and Wood took great risk leading from the front. They certainly put up a stout defense with only their sabers in hand-to-hand encounters against the Royal Scots and the Redcoats. These British veterans had years of experience as well as the advantage of the longer reach of the bayonets. General Davis held his ground at the front to stiffen his men's resolve. It was his duty to hold the British reinforcements as the army attempted an organized withdrawal. The Americans had destroyed the main batteries and achieved the goals of the sortie. Davis, along with the other American generals, refused to let their withdrawal turn into a route and stayed with their men, most of their powder wet, unable to fire back. The British, however, poured fire into

---

[232] Cruickshanks, *The Siege of Fort Erie*, 39.
[233] Barbuto, *The Canadian Theater*, 41.
[234] Barbuto, *Staff Ride Handbook for the Niagara Campaigns, 1812-1814*, 159

the Americans' ranks. Davis still refused to retreat and made a last stand to rally his men.

Crisfield Johnson's words are rousing but sad. "How gallantly they [the Americans] were led is shown by the fact that all of Porter's principal commanders were shot down—Gibson at Battery No. Two, Wood while approaching No. One, and Davis while bravely mounting a parapet between the two batteries at the head of his men."[235] He added, "The loss of these men was greatly mourned."[236]

General Davis's loyal officers were determined not to leave his body on the battlefield and carried him back to Fort Erie, described in Porter's manuscripts. "Major S. Kellogg [164th Regiment-Genesee County] likewise behaved worthy of praise, until General Davis fell near him, about the close of the action. He was then engaged in moving him off the battleground, with the assistance of Major Dunham of Colonel Crosby's [77th] Regiment. They secured their retreat with the General into our camp."[237] This is probably how General Davis's battle sword was retained and passed down to the subsequent generations of Davises in LeRoy.

The two militia majors put themselves at great risk taking the time to recover General Davis's body. "Porter's men, Miller's, and now Ripley's merged in a confused mass and started a fighting withdrawal back to Fort Erie. A musket ball passed through Ripley's neck taking him out of the fight. British-allied Indian warriors entered the fray and caught isolated Americans, smashing their heads with tomahawks. Slowly the Americans

---

[235] Johnson, 287.
[236] Babcock, 57.
[237] Cruikshank, *The Documentary History of the Campaign on the Niagara Frontier in 1814*, 232.

Brigadier General Daniel Davis and the War of 1812

exited the forest. The bloody, chaotic fight had lasted about two hours."[238]

There are two other versions detailing Daniel Davis's fate. One, a recollection of a militiaman who was not at the battle, reported in the September 21, 1859, LeRoy Gazette that a bullet pierced Daniel's jugular vein.[239] A description on page 460 of Beers agrees with a shot to the neck: "He [General Davis] led in advance of his division with sword in hand; and when warned not to ascend the parapet, did so, and was instantly and fatally shot in the neck and fell in the arms of his aide-de-camp."[240] The man who caught Daniel was Dr. Sheldon, also according to Beers. "During the War of 1812 Dr. William Sheldon was for a time captain of a militia company, but afterwards became surgeon and aide-de-camp upon the staff of General Davis and was near him when he was killed."[241] The firsthand description by Major Simon Pierson, a soldier in the War of 1812, is more convincing. Pierson's reminiscence of attending Daniel Davis's funeral was also published in the Gazette: "It was a very painful scene to witness the brave man in his coffin with his head pierced through with a ball."[242]

The six primary sources, Babcock, Barbuto, Cruikshank, Johnson, Loosing, and Whitehorne, used to compile the narrative of Daniel Davis's last days, did not mention Dr. Sheldon. But if Sheldon was nearby, it must have been a heartbreaking scene as he tried to save Daniel's life.

---

[238] Barbuto, The Canadian Theater, 41.
[239] Samson, *History of Brigadier Daniel Davis*, compiled from local sources, Reminiscences of Aaron Tufts.
[240] Beers, 460.
[241] Ibid., 74.
[242] Samson, *History of Brigadier Daniel Davis*, compiled from local sources, Recollections of Simon Pierson. (Author's note: Both recollections could be correct—If General Davis was standing on a parapet, a musket ball could have traveled through his neck and then his head, the latter wound visible at the funeral.)

General Brown considered the sortie a success, although the Americans had lost many good men, including senior officers. In a letter he wrote to Governor Thompkins, General Brown said, "The militia of New York have redeemed their character—they behaved gallantly. Thus in barely two hours the result attempted had been achieved, the enemy irreparably crippled, and one thousand [British] men killed, injured, or taken prisoners."[243]

Four days after the sortie, the British retreated to the north of the Chippewa River. It was ironic that the Americans discovered later that the British had made plans to lift the siege before the sortie, but the attack by the Americans weakened the enemy. The British and their Mohawk allies would not invade nor terrorize western New York again.

---

[243] Babcock, 64.

CHAPTER XVI: The War Ends

On December 24, 1814, representatives of the United States and Britain signed a peace treaty in Ghent, Belgium, to end the War of 1812. Unfortunately, before word reached North America, on January 8, 1815, the British attacked New Orleans. In the resulting battle, General Andrew Jackson defeated the British invasion force. President Madison signed the Treaty of Ghent on February 18, 1815. In the terms of the treaty, the borders of the United States and Canada reverted back to pre-war status. In addition, the British stopped their military support of the Native Americans, ended trade restrictions, and halted the impressment of U.S. sailors.

As had happened after the American Revolution, the Native Americans were not part of the treaty of the War of 1812. They lost more of their lands and became more vulnerable to future depredations. The effort of the United States to annex its neighbor during the war instead united the Canadians and planted the seed of an independent Canada. Babcock wrote in 1899, "And while the history of our brave [American] men is written, let due praise be accorded to our former foes, who, through the mutation of time and circumstance, are now our nearest neighbors and best friends."[244]

---

[244] Babcock 64

Michael A. Ponzio

In October 1814, the people of Genesee County welcomed home their men released from militia duty and grieved those who had given their lives for their country. Major Simon Pierson of LeRoy, who attended Daniel Davis's funeral, published his recollections in the March 28, 1856, LeRoy Gazette. "The remains of General Davis were brought home. The writer attended the funeral. It was a very painful scene to witness the brave man in his coffin with his head pierced through with a ball, with his children and other relatives bewailing their loss. He was buried with military honors near Jeremiah Buell's place, LeRoy. He was a brave officer and was killed at the sortie at Fort Erie, age 37 years. His descendants were Alfred, Asher, [d. before 1814] deceased, David, Leveritt, Samuel and a daughter [Naomi]. His widow [Naomi Le Barron Davis] and family moved to [Ypsilanti] Michigan many years since.[245]

The cemetery where his family buried General Davis was known as the old cemetery east of the village, Limerock Cemetery, and eventually Buell Cemetery. The land for the burial ground, the first in LeRoy, was on land owned by the Buell family. His son, Captain Asa Porter Buell, an officer in Daniel's brigade, was also killed during the sortie on September 17, 1814. He is buried there as well as generations of the Buell family. Dr. William Sheldon, aide-de-camp to Daniel at the siege of Fort Erie, was also buried in the cemetery many years later when he died in 1873.

General Daniel Davis was praised by his senior officer in a letter describing the sortie from Fort Erie.

---

[245] Samson, John P., *History of Brigadier Daniel Davis*, Recollections of Simon Pierson.

Brigadier General Daniel Davis and the War of 1812

From Brigadier General Porter to Major General Brown. Fort Erie, September 23rd, 1814:

> "... *in taking the second battery, the gallant leaders of the three divisions all fell nearly at the same time: Colonel Gibson at the second battery, and General Davis and Lieutenant-Colonel Wood in an assault upon the first. Brigadier-General Davis, although a militia officer of little experience, conducted himself on this occasion with all the coolness and bravery of a veteran, and fell while advancing upon the enemy's entrenchments. His loss as a citizen as well as a soldier will be severely felt in the patriotic county of Genesee.*"[246]

In his history of the Niagara Campaign, author Richard V. Barbuto[247] mentions General Davis with distinction: "State militias saw much more success in 1814 than in previous years [of the War of 1812]. Brown could not have attacked the British batteries without the hundreds of New York militiamen who waived their constitutional rights and volunteered to cross the Niagara to save the soldiers in beleaguered Fort Erie. Militia generals, such as Porter and Davis, led from the front and inspired their men."[248]

In a speech on September 20, 1814, President Madison and Congress recognized the U.S. Army's defense of the country without due respect for the militia's contribution. To

---

[246] Cruikshank, *The Documentary History of the Campaign on the Niagara Frontier in 1814, Part II*, 208.

[247] The Author Richard V. Barbuto holds a Ph.D. in history from the University of Kansas and is a professor and deputy director of the Department of Military History at the U.S. Army Command and General Staff College. He served twenty-three years as an armor officer before retiring from the U.S. Army in 1994.

[248] Barbuto, 57.

compensate for the president's lack of respect, the New York Senate, urged by Governor Tompkins, passed a bill on October 10, 1814, to honor twelve officers (militiamen and U.S. Army regulars), deserving special recognition for their service within the state of New York. State representatives presented the honorees, or if posthumous, a family member, with an ornate sword.

Four of the recipients were soldiers in the New York State Militia. Six of the recipients fought in the Siege of Fort Erie alongside Daniel Davis. One of the twelve honored officers was the late Brigadier General Daniel Davis.

The forward of the New York State resolution that addressed the honored men stated, "That this Legislature deplore the loss of Brigadier-General Davis, of the militia of this State, who fell in the sortie from Fort Erie, and present his eldest male heir with a sword."[249]

The following letter from Governor Tomkins was sent to Daniel's oldest son, Alfred Davis, in December 1814:[250]

---

[249] Hamilton, *A Roland for an Oliver Swords Awarded by the State of New York During the War of 1812*, 6.
[250] Tompkins, *Public Papers of Daniel D. Tompkins, Governor of New York, 1807-1817, Volume 3*, 631.

Brigadier General Daniel Davis and the War of 1812

A SWORD PRESENTED TO THE SON OF GENERAL DAVIS WHO WAS KILLED AT FORT ERIE.

New York, December 24, 1814.

Sir: You will perceive by the enclosed document that the Senate & Assembly of the State of New York are sensible of the distinguished merit & conduct of your lamented Father, Brigadier General Davis, in the sortie from Fort Erie, & sincerely deplore his death. They have charged me to present to you a sword as a mark of public gratitude for his generous & gallant services. I shall hasten to convey to you the memorial which a grateful people consecrate to the memory of one of their most illustrious defenders. I beseech you to bear in mind that it is the need of patriotism & of virtuous self devotion & should ever a crisis arise, which shall require you to unsheath it, emulate the deeds of your heroic sire, & think no sacrifice too great in the cause of a beloved country. May you follow his footsteps in the path of virtue & of glory, & be prosperous & happy.

I am with great regard, Your most Ob't. & Hble. Servt.

Daniel D. Tompkins.

To Alfred Davis, eldest male heir of the late Brigadier General Daniel Davis* of the New York Militia.

On March 4, 1817, the sword was presented to Alfred Davis, eldest son of Brigadier General Daniel Davis. Where is this sword? What did it look like? And what about Daniel's battle sword he held when he fell in the sortie from Fort Erie? What was the destiny of the two swords?

Michael A. Ponzio

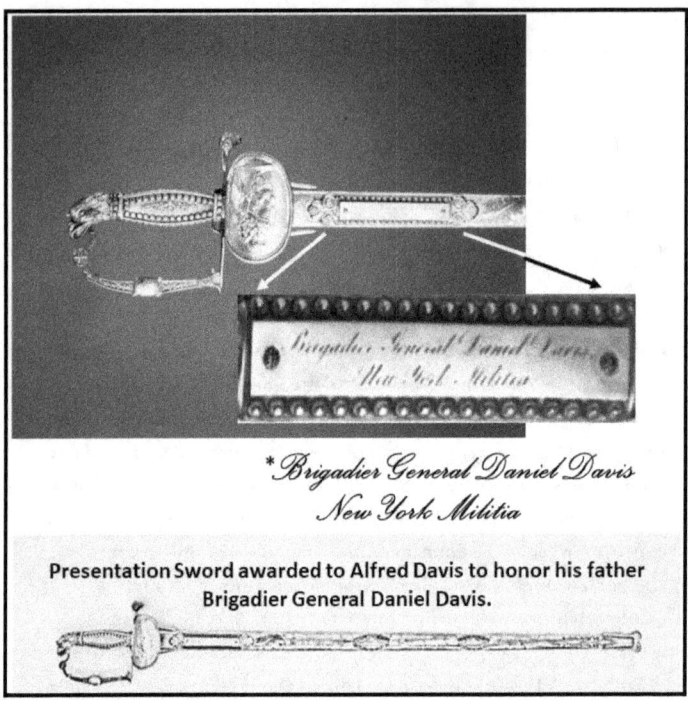

[251] PD-US-expired. This work is in the public domain in its country of origin and other countries and areas where the copyright term is the author's life plus 100 years or fewer.

---

[251] Presentation Sword and Scabbard of Brigadier General Daniel Davis (1777–1814) of the New York Militia ca. 1815–17, The Met.

CHAPTER XVII: The Destiny of the Two Swords

On March 4, 1817, Alfred Davis was sixteen when he accepted the sword honoring his late father Brigadier Daniel Davis. Alfred was considered an adult and had assumed the management of the Davis farm, on the north side of present-day East Main, in LeRoy. Certainly his mother, Naomi, and his family were present for this ceremony. Did a New York state representative bring the sword to their homestead? An appropriate location for the presentation of the sword would have been where Daniel was buried, at Buell Cemetery, only a mile west of the Daniel Davis farm.

Daniel's other children would have been at the ceremony: Naomi, 17; David, 10; Leveritt, 8; and Samuel, 3. Daniel's brother James Jr., who lived across the road, would have been there, accompanied by his wife Jehannah, and their four children: Lewis, 17; Edan, 13; Ezra, 5; and Hamlet, less than a year old.

Daniel's sister Lydia and her husband might have been present, but their place of residence is unknown. However, Norton S. Davis, Daniel's youngest brother, likely attended. He lived on his farm less than a half mile east of James Davis's homestead.

Others that lived in LeRoy who were certainly at the presentation would have been Dr. William Sheldon, Major

Simon Pierson, Major Benjamin Ganson, and probably John Buell, father of Asa, who was killed in battle alongside Daniel.

The presentation sword, made by John Targee, a silversmith in New York City from 1795 to 1807, was eventually donated to the New York Metropolitan Museum. The sword's description by the museum states, "The sword's design reflects the classical inspiration of the Federal period. The hilt, with its downturned shell, is based on French Empire models. The image of Hercules and the Nemean Lion, emblematic of strength and courage, is probably copied from an English engraving after a classical gem or cameo. The eagle-headed pommel, on the other hand, is typically American, as is the style of engraving on the scabbard, illustrating the battle."[252]

The sword was inscribed with: Brigadier General Daniel Davis, New York Militia. "Engraved on the scabbard: *As a testimonial of the high sense entertained of the services and gallantry of Brigadier General Daniel Davis, particularly in the Sortie at Erie where he fell leading his fellow Citizens to victory, this Sword is presented by his Excellency Daniel D [Tompkins].*"[253]

How did the sword become a treasured piece at the Metropolitan Museum? Alfred Davis moved to Ypsilanti, Michigan, by 1825, according to a record of his marriage in that year. The sword remained in the family until 1921. It was then purchased by Summer Healey and subsequently sold for $200 to Francis P. Gavan, who donated it to the New York Metropolitan Museum in 1922.

The record of the presentation sword awarded to Alfred Davis by the State of New York is well documented, but what happened to General Davis's battle sword? When Majors Kellogg and Dunham carried the general's body off the

---

[252] Presentation Sword and Scabbard of Brigadier General Daniel Davis, The Met.
[253] Ibid. ('Daniel D'. Tompkins, Governor of New York).

battlefield, they must have certainly retrieved his sword as well. Daniel's family was fortunate. Not all of the fallen were recovered, although "most of the American officers who were killed were returned by the British for burial at home, and vice versa, according to the military practice of the time."[254]

General Daniel Davis's battle sword is a saber with a curved blade, a one-handed weapon with a single cutting edge. The white handle, made of bone, is textured, and with a brass loop guard. Floral patterns, a cannon, and a lightning bolt of gold leaf decorate the sword. The groove or fuller is relatively wide, making the blade lightweight.

When the image of the handle was entered in the *Oldswords.com* database, the closest match showed it was very similar to the style crafted for high-ranking French officers between 1800 to 1821, which includes the period of General Davis's military career as an officer. He began as a lieutenant in 1801 and made captain by 1803. He was promoted to major in 1805, to lieutenant colonel the next year, and full colonel in 1809. In 1814 when General Rea passed away, the governor appointed Daniel to lead the 6th Brigade as Brigadier General. He likely purchased his battle sword in 1805 or later, considering the commitment and monetary investment.

---

[254] Many were not so fortunate. During the reconstruction of Old Fort Erie in 1937, workers found a mass grave of 150 British and three American soldiers. Accounts mention Americans dug a mass grave outside the fort for the soldiers who fell during the assault on Fort Erie in 1814. A monument was erected for the fallen. In 1988, a backhoe turned up bones beside Snake Hill, where a battle took place on Aug. 14, 1814. Canada undertook an archeological dig, uncovering the remains of 28 American soldiers. The remains were taken to a veterans' cemetery at Bath, N.Y., where a full military funeral was held before reburial. Bath was chosen because of archival evidence that many of those who fought at Fort Erie were militiamen from the Finger Lakes region of upstate New York.   Burns, *After 174 Years, 28 M.I.A.'s Return.*

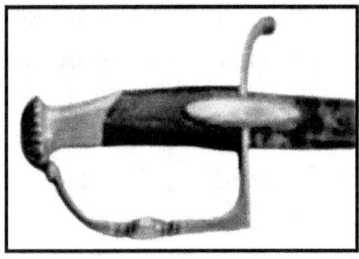 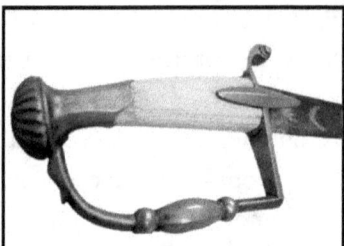

French officer's sword   Davis sword

Results using the computer data base of "Oldswords" https://oldswords.com indicated that Brigadier General Davis's battle sword closely matched Senior French Army officers' swords of the period 1800-1821.

> SOURCE: https://oldswords.com/ The site is designed to help collectors identify swords in their collections. It is the largest online resource of its type on the Internet and has been successfully assisting collectors identify swords for nearly 10 years.
>
> The site has approx. 55,000 images of over 6,500 swords. Over 700 recognizable models/patterns and a gallery consisting of over 300 official/government patterns from 21 different nations.

The Two Swords

In 2001, **Alfred** C. "Chopper" **Davis**, US Army Veteran, **son of Daniel Davis**, US Air Force Veteran, inherited General Davis's *battle sword* from his father, who passed away. It had been kept in the family since 1814. Chopper donated the sword to the LeRoy Historical Society on July 2, 2022.

In 1817, **Alfred Davis, son of Daniel Davis**, was given a *presentation sword* by the State of New York, to honor his father, Brigadier General Davis, who was killed in battle in 1814. The sword is now at the New York Metropolitan Museum.

Color images of the swords are on this book's cover.

Michael A. Ponzio

Original tombstone in Buell Cemetery of Brigadier General Daniel Davis

Brigadier General Daniel Davis and the War of 1812

SACRED TO THE MEMORY OF
BRIG GEN DANIEL DAVIS
OF THE N Y MILITIA
WHO WAS KILLED BACK OF FORT ERIE
AT THE SORTIE FROM THE FORT
ON THE 17 SEP. 1814
AGED 37 YRS

Second tombstone added in 1997 by
Franklin Davis of LeRoy, N.Y.
and James M. Davis of Seneca, S.C.
Descendants of Brigadier General Daniel Davis

Secure he stood his front undaunted shows,

And bravely fought amidst a host of foes.

Far more than death he feared a sull , d name

and now he ,/s fallen his days are closed with fame.

Oh wide destroying death thou pale affright,

How couldst thou take this hero from our sight.

Michael A. Ponzio

**Excerpt from the 1805 Deed Purchased by Daniel Davis
100 acre Lot 26 for $300.**
(Source: United States Land Records 1630-1975, Deeds 1792-1807, Vol. 1-2.)

- Daniel Davis Lot 26
- 100 acres
- "East Main"
- "year one thousand eight hundred and five"
- County of Genesee
- Daniel Davis of Caledonia
- Daniel paid "three hundred dollars"

The official name for the town where Daniel Davis's farm was located was Caledonia (The name LeRoy was adopted in 1813).

Brigadier General Daniel Davis and the War of 1812

Land Assessment of Daniel Davis's Lot 26 in 1805

Grantee's Name	Event Date	Event Place	Grantor's Name	Event Type	Entry Number	Page Number
Daniel Davis	1805	Genesee, NY US	James Pulteney	Land Assessment	7	284

Genesee County was part of Ontario County until 1803

SOURCE: United States, New York Land Records, 1630-1975;
https://familysearch.org/ark:/61903/3:1:3QS7-89WX-69M1-Y?cc=2078654&wc=M7HP-H38%3A358135801%2C358171801

Michael A. Ponzio

Brigadier General Daniel Davis Timeline

- 1776: February 23: Daniel Davis is born in Killingworth, Connecticut.

- 1779: Daniel's father, James Sr., likely fought with the Killingworth militia at Tryon's raid in New Haven during the American Revolution.

- 1799: Daniel Davis and Philemon Nettleton journey to present day Lime Rock (three miles east of Oatka Creek on the east side of LeRoy) and make improvements to land purchased by Daniel. They build a log house on Daniel's land at Limerock.

- Between 1799 and April 9, 1800: Daniel Davis and Philemon Nettleton returned to Killingworth, Connecticut, and return to Lime Rock with friends and their families. In the family of Mr. Nettleton was Miss Naomi Le Barron, a sister of Mrs. Nettleton. The Davis and Nettleton families move to Lime Rock. Daniel Davis's father, James Davis, Sr., and Daniel's mother, Hannah, and four of their children live north of the road ("East Main") in Lime Rock.

- April 9, 1800: Lewis Davis is born in Ganson's Settlement (present day LeRoy), the first child of James Davis Jr. (Daniel's older brother by two years) and Jehannah Wilcox Davis.

- 1800 Autumn: The first marriages are held in Ganson's Settlement, when Daniel Davis and Naomi Le Barron and Gardner Carver and Lydia Davis were married. (Lydia was Daniel's sister).
- 1801: Daniel Davis was chosen a *pathmaster*, whose job it is to maintain public paths and roads.
- 1801: The first military training west of the Genesee River is held in Ganson Settlement in 1801. As in some parts of western New York, in Genesee County, enlisted militiamen brought a tradition from New England of electing their non-commissioned officers, lieutenants, and captains. The militiamen choose Joseph Hewitt as captain and Daniel Davis as lieutenant.
- 1803: Daniel Davis is promoted to captain in a regiment to be composed of the militia of Genesee County, reporting to Lt. Colonel Alexander Rae.
- 1804: A meeting is called to organize a school district. Daniel Davis is elected as the chairman. The committee had the first frame schoolhouse built west of the Genesee River, replacing the original log schoolhouse built in 1801.
- 1805: Daniel Davis is promoted to major, commanding a battalion in General Alex Rea's regiment.
- 1806: General Rea's militia is expanded into a brigade and the brigade divided into three regiments. Daniel Davis is

promoted to Lieutenant Colonel commanding one of the new regiments. (77th NY Militia)

- 1806: James Davis, Jr., builds a log cabin across the road from the Davis family farm.
- 1807: Daniel Davis inherits his father's farm at Lime Rock and builds a frame house.
- 1807: Daniel Davis is an early tavern keeper.
- 1808: Daniel Davis is made a Mason in Genesee lodge Avon, New York, "sometime between September 7, 1808, and December 27, 1812".
- 1809: Daniel Davis is promoted to colonel in the militia.
- 1813: Tuscarora Iroquois warriors defend Americans fleeing Lewiston, a village along the Niagara River, burned by British – Tuscarora fugitives camp at Lime Rock, near or on Daniel Davis's farm.
- 1814: March 2 – Daniel Davis is appointed Brigadier General of the 6th brigade, New York State militia infantry, replacing Alexander Rea (deceased).
- 1814: Sept. 3 – New York Governor Thompson requests volunteers to defend the Niagara Frontier. Brigadier General Davis of Genesee County orders out his whole brigade.
- 1814: September 10 – Brigadier General Daniel Davis leads two regiments (77th and 164th) of his brigade across the Niagara River to reinforce Fort Erie.

- 1814: September 17 – In the sortie which broke the siege of Fort Erie, Daniel Davis leads one of the columns to destroy the British batteries, is shot as he fought at the front of his men and dies on the battlefield. Major S. Kellogg and Major Dunham, both officers in Daniel's Genesee County brigade, carry him off the battleground, to the militia camp at Fort Erie, during the American retreat.
- 1814: Brigadier Daniel Davis is buried at Buell Cemetery in Lime Rock near his farm.
- 1814: December 24 – Letter of recognition from Governor Tompkins. Presentation Sword to honor Brigadier General Daniel Davis given to his oldest son, Alfred Davis, on March 4, 1817.
- 1815: Colonel Worthy Churchill is appointed Brigadier General of the 6th New York Militia Brigade Genesee County in place of the late Brigadier General Daniel Davis.

Brigadier General Daniel Davis and the War of 1812
The Destiny of the Two Swords

Thank you for purchasing this book. I know you could have picked any number of books to read, but you picked this book and for that I am extremely grateful.

I hope that it added interest, knowledge, and entertainment to your everyday life. If so, it would be appreciated if you could share this book with your friends and family and post comments on Facebook and Twitter.

If you enjoyed this book and found some benefit in reading this, I'd like to hear from you and hope that you could take some time to post a review on Amazon. Your feedback and support will help this author to improve.

I want you, the reader, to know that your review is very important and if you'd like to *leave a review on Amazon, search the book on Amazon Books by its title or my name.*

Amazon's Michael A. Ponzio Author Page
Amazon.com: Michael A. Ponzio: Books, Biography, Blog, Audiobooks, Kindle

Michael A Ponzio Author Facebook:
https://www.facebook.com/AncestryNovels/?ref=bookmarks

Author's Ancestry Novels website:
History & Historical Fiction: Pontius, Ponzio, Pons, and Ponce
https://mikemarianoponzio.wixsite.com/pontius-ponzio-pons

Michael A. Ponzio

ABOUT THE AUTHOR

Since childhood, Mike Ponzio has read about history, trading books and stories with his father, Joseph E. Ponzio. Mike traveled around the Mediterranean to Europe, Asia, and Africa, visiting many of the locations which would inspire him to write *Ancestry Novels* which he imagines may have taken place during the lives of ancient ancestors.

Mike's wife, Anne Davis and her Davis family, descended from General Davis, inspired Mike to write *Brigadier General Daniel Davis and the War of 1812, The Destiny of the Two Swords,* the first book of nonfiction history he has authored.

Mike met his wife, Anne Davis, in 1975 at a University of Florida karate class. Since that time both have taught Cuong Nhu Martial Arts. With John Burns, they wrote and published six instructional books on martial arts weapons. Mike retired in 2015, after working as an environmental engineer for thirty-seven years. Anne and Mike have raised four sons, who are also engineer graduates, following in the footsteps of their Davis and Ponzio grandfathers.

Ancestry Novels by Michael A. Ponzio.

The Ancient Rome Series:
Pontius Aquila: Eagle of the Republic
Pontius Pilatus: Dark Passage to Heaven
Saint Pontianus: Bishop of Rome

Warriors and Monks Series:
Ramon Pons: Count of Toulouse
1066 Sons of Pons: In the Wake of the Conqueror
Warriors and Monks: Pons, Abbot of Cluny

Lantern Across the Sea: The Genoese Arbalester

BIBLIOGRAPHY

1. *A Piece of New York State History Captured in Monument to Honor Tuscaroras for Help in Battle*, Associated Press, Lewiston, NY, Jan. 03, 2019, https://www.silive.com/news/2013/04/a_piece_of_new_york_state_hist.html#:~:text=Instead%2C%20a%20larger-than-life%20bronze%20monument%20will%20permanently%20recall,invading%20British-Canadian%20forces%20who%20were%20burning%20it%20down, accessed 5-1-2022.

2. American Revolution 07/03/1779 - *Battles - Tryon's Raid in Connecticut Begins* (Naval Battle), RevWarTalk, https://www.revwartalk.com/07-03-1779-battles-tryon-s-raid-in-connecticut-begins-naval-battle/, accessed 2-28-2022.

3. Babcock, Louis L., *The Siege of Fort Erie: An Episode of the War of 1812*, The Peter Paul Book Company, Buffalo, 1899.

4. *"Baby walkers, standing stools, antique go-arts, baby runners, walking stools, trainers"*, Old & Interesting History of Domestic Paraphernalia, oldandinteresting.com, accessed 2-25-2022.

5. Bailey, Rev. Frederick W., *"Early Connecticut Marriages as found on Ancient Church Records Prior to 1800, Vol 4"*, 2nd Church of Killingworth, org. 18 Jan 1738, dunhamwilcox.net/ct/2kill_marr_grm.htm, accessed 2-28-2022.

6. Barber, Jedediah, *"Homer Grows Rapidly in the 1800s"*, 2019 Town of Homer,

NY.https://townofhomer.org/about-the-town-of-homer/history-of-homer-ny/homer-grows-rapidly-in-the-1800s/, accessed 3-20-2022.

7. Barbuto, Richard V. , *Staff Ride Handbook for the Niagara Campaigns, 1812-1814,* Combat Studies Institute Press, US Army Combined Arms Center, Fort Leavenworth, Kansas, https://www.armyupress.army.mil/Portals/7/educational-services/staff-rides/StaffRideHB_NiagaraCampaign1812-1814.pdf

8. Barbuto, Lt. Col. Richard V., The Canadian Theater 1814, CMH Pub 74–6, Center of Military History, United States Army, Washington, D.C., 2014.

9. Barbuto, Lt. Col. Richard V., The War of 1812 on the Niagara River, The Army Historical Foundation (AHF), The Campaign for the National Museum of the United States Army, https://armyhistory.org/the-war-of-1812-on-the-niagara-river/, accessed 4-26-2022.

10. Barbuto, Lt. Col. Richard V, *Staff Ride Handbook for the Niagara Campaigns, 1812-1814,* Combat Studies Institute Press US Army Combined Arms Center Fort Leavenworth, Kansas, https://www.armyupress.army.mil/Portals/7/educational-services/staff-rides/StaffRideHB_NiagaraCampaign1812-1814.pdf

11. Beers, F.W., *Gazetteer and Biographical Source No. 1: Record of Genesee County, N.Y. 1788-1890,* J. W. Vose & Co. Publishers, Syracuse, N.Y., 1890.

12. Bell, J.L., *"The British Soldiers Weren't Called Lobsterbacks",* Boston 1775 History, analysis, and unabashed gossip

about the start of the American Revolution in Massachusetts, 11-5-2007, accessed 2-27-2022.

13. Bellis, Mary. "History of the Plow." ThoughtCo, Feb. 16, 2021, thoughtco.com/history-of-the-plow-1992324.

14. Belluscio, Lynne, *"200 Years of Settlement"*, LeRoy Historical Society Newsletter, Vol.8, No.2, 1997."

15. Belluscio, Lynne, J., *"Images of America"*, Arcadia Publishing, 2010, Charleston, SC, Chicago, Ill.

16. Belluscio, Lynne, *"Ganson's Tavern"*, LeRoy Pennysaver, August 9, 2009.

17. Belluscio, Lynne, *June 8, 1812-2012, Our Bicentennial*, LeRoy Pennysaver, September 11, 2011

18. Berton, Pierre, *Flames Across the Border, 1813-1814*. Westminster, London, England, Penguin Books, 1988.

19. Bills, Joe, *"The Camden Toboggan Chute"*, https://newengland.com/yankee-magazine/travel/maine/camden-toboggan-chute-up-close/, January 6, 2016, accessed 2-18-2022.

20. *Books That Shaped America* | Exhibitions - Library of Congress (loc.gov), https://www.loc.gov/exhibits/books-that-shaped-america/1750-to-1800.htm, accessed 3-6-2022.

21. Bridenbaugh, Carl, *"The New England Town: A Way of Life"*, (American Antiquarian Society),(americanantiquarian.org), accessed 2-18-2022.

22. Britannica, T. Editors of Encyclopaedia. "Niagara-on-the-Lake." *Encyclopedia Britannica*, February 24, 2016. https://www.britannica.com/place/Niagara-on-the-Lake.

23. Britannica, T. Editors of Encyclopaedia. "public house." Encyclopedia Britannica, July 22, 2021. https://www.britannica.com/topic/public-house.

24. Burns, John F., After 174 Years, 28 M.I.A.'s Return, The New York Times, July 1, 1988, https://www.nytimes.com/1988/07/01/world/after-174-years-28-mia-s-return.html#:~:text=Many%20in%20the,their%20war%20dead., accessed 6-5-2022.

25. Caledonia-First-Presbyterian-Church-Prayer-Profile.pdf (myworshiptimes22.com),https://media.myworshiptimes22.com/wp-content/uploads/sites/25/2020/05/05151151/Caledonia-First-Presbyterian-Church-Prayer-Profile.pdf accessed 3-23-2022

26. Carly, Rachel, Lebanon, *Connecticut Historical and Architectural Resources Inventory 2013*, Town of Lebanon Connecticut State Historic Preservation Office, https://www.lebanonct.gov/sites/g/files/vyhlif4596/f/uploads/2013_lebanon_historical_and_architectural_r esources_inventory_introduction.pdf.

27. Chaisson, Bill, *"The Fabled History of Apples"*, Ithaca.com, Sep 18, 2013 Updated Oct 1, 2014 https://www.ithaca.com/special_sections/the-fabled-history-of-apples/article_1b26b9b0-209f-11e3-bc1e-001a4bcf887a.html, accessed 4-1-2022.

28. Chazanof, William, *Joseph Ellicott and the Holland Land Company: The Opening of Western New York*, Syracuse University Press, 1970.

29. Cole, Frank Thoedore, Ed., *The Old Northwest Genealogical Quarterly, Vol. 12,* 1909, Columbus, Ohio.

30. Colley, Brent M., *The Farms of Redding, Connecticut, and Colonial Farming Pag*e, historyofredding.net, accessed 3-17-2022.

31. Cruikshank, Lt. Colonel Ernest Alexander, *The Documentary History of the Campaign on the Niagara Frontier in 1814, Part II,* Edited for the Lundy's Lane Historical Society, Printed at the Tribune Office, Welland, 1896.

32. Cruikshank, Captain K., *The Siege of Fort Erie, August 1st-September 23rd, 1814,* Lundy Lane Historical Society, Printed at the Tribune Office, Welland, 1906.

33. Cunnigham, Janice P., *Connecticut's Agricultural Heritage, An Architectural and Historical Overview, Connecticut Trust for Historical Preservation, Historic barns of Connecticut*, April 2012, https://connecticutbarns.org/images/uploads/Connecticuts%20Agricultural%20Heritage%20Report_final2012-0512.pdf, accessed 3-17-2022.

34. "*Davis/Davies/David", Background,* Family Tree DNA, www.familytreedna.com/groups/davis/about/background, accessed 3-1-2022.

35. Davis, Betty Neracker, "*James M. Davis Family Geological records compiled by Betty Neracker Davis*, Seneca, S.C. 2006.

36. Davis, Alfred C. "Chopper," *Interview, May 2022.*

37. Davis, Franklin, *Interview*, April 2022.

38. Davis, Mary Ann Bovee Davis, *Obituary, Buell Cemetery*, https://www.findagrave.com/memorial/61631328/mary-ann-davis, accessed 4-5-2022.

39. De Melker, Saska, *"Agrarian roots? Think again. Debunking the myth of summer vacation's origins"*, PBS NewsHour Weekend, 9-7-2014, accessed 3-6-2022. 2-27-2022.

40. Dexter, Franklin Bowditch, *Biographical Sketches of the Graduates of Yale College*, Vol.4 1778-1792, New York Henry Holt Co., 1907. Pg. 89.

41. Earle, Alice Morse, *The Sabbath in Puritan New England*, Gutenberg Project eBook8659, 2014 https://www.reformedreader.org/puritans/sabbath.puritan.newengland/sabbath.puritan.newengland.chapter8.htm.

42. Ellis, David Maldwyn, *"The Yankee Invasion of New York, 1783-1850." New York History* 32, no. 1 (1951): 3–17. http://www.jstor.org/stable/23149993. accessed 3-6-2022. 3-11-2022.

43. Enfilade, *Mirriam-Webster Dictionary*, https://www.merriam-webster.com/dictionary/enfilade.

44. Esch, John J., *Our Second Line: The National Guard*, The North American Review, Aug., 1903, Vol. 177, No. 561 (Aug., 1903), pp. 288- 296 Published by: University of Northern Iowa, https://www.jstor.org/stable/25119440, accessed 3-6-2022. 5-14-2022.

45. *Family Life*, Colonial America Reference Library,

https://www.encyclopedia.com/history/encyclopedias-almanacs-transcripts-and-maps/family-life, accessed 3-6-2022. 3-11-2022.

46. Foley, Janet Wethy, *Early Settlers of New York State: Their Ancestors and Descendants, Part One, Vol. I-III.*, 1934, Akron, NY, reprint 2007, Heritage, Westminster, Maryland.

47. Ford, Dixon and Kreutzer, Lee, "*Oxen: Engines of Overland Emigration*", Overland Journal, Vol.33, No.1 Spring 2015, https://www.nps.gov/cali/learn/historyculture/upload/OJ-spring2015-oxen.pdf, accessed 3-18-22.

48. Gade, Carla, Literacy in Colonial America, June 15, 2011, ColonialQuills, https://colonialquills.blogspot.com/2011/06/literacy-in-colonial-america.html, accessed 3-6-2022.

49. Gerlander, Todd L. Captain, "Understanding the Connecticut Militia During the Revolution", Connecticut Society of the American Revolution, https://www.connecticutsar.org/ accessed 3-6-2022.

50. Gray, Vickie, LeRoy Town, Genesee County, New York Genweb Project, *Brief History of town of LeRoy*, https://sites.rootsweb.com/~nycleroy/TownsOfGeneseeCounty/History-LeRoy.htm, accessed 3-18-2022.

51. Greene, Nelson, ed. *History of the Mohawk Valley: Gateway to the West 1614-1925, Vol. II Chapter 8*, S. J. Clarke Publishing Company, 1925.

52. *Groove swords not blood groove*, Vintage News, https://www.thevintagenews.com/2016/08/11/groove-swords-not-blood-grove/?edg-c=1

53. Hamilton, John D., *A Roland for an Oliver Swords Awarded by the State of New York During the War of 1812*, 4. American Society of Arms Collectors, Bulletin No.57, Fall 1984. https://americansocietyofarmscollectors.org/articles/

54. Hammersley, Col. Syndey Ernest, *The History of Waterford, New York*, Published by Theo, Gaus' Sons, Inc., Brooklyn, N.Y., 1957.

55. Hall, Ellery L. "Canadian Annexation Sentiment in Kentucky Prior to the War of 1812." *Register of Kentucky State Historical Society* 28, no. 85 (1930): 372–80. http://www.jstor.org/stable/23370018.1

56. Hauptman, Laurence M., "They Also Served: American Indian Women in the War of 1812", Magazine of Smithsonian's National Museum of the American Indian, Fall 2015, Vol. 16, No.3, https://www.americanindianmagazine.org/story/they-also-served-american-indian-women-war-1812

57. Harland-Jacobs, Jessica, *Handbook of Freemasonry*, Ch 24, FreemasonryandColonialism, https://doi.org/10.1163/9789004273122_025

58. Herzog, Carl, Public Historian, "*Slavery and the USS Constitution*", USS Constitution Museum, June 19, 2020, https://ussconstitutionmuseum.org/2020/06/19/slavery-and-uss-constitution/

59. Horn, Dr. David, "History of the First Congregational Church of Hamilton Meetinghouses", A Story of God's Faithfulness, First Congregational Church of Hamilton, FCCH publication, 2014. https://hwlibrary.org/wp-

content/uploads/2020/11/FCCH-hist.-11-10.pdf, accessed 2-18-2022.

60. Hotchkin, Rev. James Hervey, "A History of the Purchase and Settlement of Western New York, and of the Rise, Progress, and Present State of the Presbyterian Church in that Section", Published by M. W: Dodd, New York, 1848.

61. Howell, Austin Gage, Weapons in the War of 1812, North Carolina State University, 2013, NCpedia, https://www.ncpedia.org/weapons-war-1812, 4-5-2022.

62. Hyman, Tony, Cigar History 1762-1862 U.S. Cigar Industry Begins Cigar History Museum © Tony Hyman, all rights reserved 05-18-17, accessed 4-1-2022.

63. Jenkins, Edward H., *A History of Connecticut Agriculture*, New Haven: Connecticut Agricultural Experiment Station, 1925.

64. Johnson, Crisfield, and Joseph Meredith Toner Collection. *Centennial history of Erie County, New York: being its annals from the earliest recorded events to the hundredth year of American independence.* Buffalo, N. Y.: Printing House of Matthews & Warren, 1876. Web. https://lccn.loc.gov/01014083.

65. Johnston, Henry P. A.M., *The Record of Connecticut Men in the Military and Naval Service During the War of the Revolution 1775-1783*, Under the Authority of the Adjutant-General of Connecticut, Hartford,1889. https://archive.org/details/waroftherevolution00recorich/page/n41/mode/2up?view=theater&q=war, accessed 3-3-2022.

66. Killingworth Historical Marker, *"First Settlers of the Second Society"*, Killingworth Historical Marker (hmdb.org). accessed 2-18-2022.

67. LaChiusa, Chuck, *"History of Buffalo, 1800"*, Buffalo 1800-1831 (buffaloah.com),3-15-22.

68. Lapham's Quarterly, Jemison, https://www.laphamsquarterly.org/contributors/Jemison, accessed 3-13-2022.

69. Lentz, Thomas L. *"History of The Congregational Church in Killingworth"*, History of The Congregational Church in Killingworth | HKNow (hk-now.com), 2-19-2020.

70. LeRoy, New York Historical Marker, *Herman LeRoy's Mill HistoricalMarker*, https://www.hmdb.org/m.asp?m=142118., accessed 3-21-2022.

71. Lossing, Benson, J., Lossing's Field Book of the War of 1812,

72. Lockridge, Kenneth A., *Literacy in Colonial America, An Enquiry into the Social Context of Literacy in the Early Modern West*, W. W. Norton & Company; January 17, 1975.

73. Lusk, J. (2011). *Mediation and Middlemen Undone: The Demise of the Colonial Go-Between in Revolutionary New York* (Master's thesis, Duquesne University). Retrieved from https://dsc.duq.edu/etd/844.

74. Mansfield, J. B., ed., *History of the Great Lakes. Volume I*, A transcription for the Maritime History of the Great Lakes site by Walter Lewis and Brendon Baillod, Halton Hills, ON, Canada: Maritime History of the Great Lakes, 2003.,

75. https://www.maritimehistoryofthegreatlakes.ca/documents/hgl/default.asp?ID=c011, accessed 4-21-2022.

76. Mays, D A (2004). *Women in Early America: Struggle, Survival, and Freedom in a New World.* Santa Barbara, CA: ABC-CLIO.

77. McClure, George. *"Gen. McClure's further relation of facts. To the public. Canandaigua, 1814."*, Library of Congress, Pdf. https://www.loc.gov/item/rbpe.11401700/. accessed 4-26-2022.

78. McIntosh, W. H., Prof., *History of Wayne County, New York 1789-1877*, Everts, Ensign & Everts, Press of J.B. Lippincott & Co. Philadelphia, 1877.

79. *Military Minutes of the Council of Appointment:1783-1821*, Volume 1 -2, Annual Reports of the State Historian, Genesee County.

80. Miller, Martha M, *"Part I: Chapter 7. "Clothing and Consumers in Rural New England, 1760-1810". The Needle's Eye: "Women and Work in the Age of Revolution."*, ScholarWorks@UMass Amherst, 2006.

81. "Winfield Scott," *New World Encyclopedia*, https://www.newworldencyclopedia.org/p/index.php?title=Winfield_Scott&oldid=1043653 (accessed May 16, 2022).

82. *Niagara Falls History, the Battle of Queenston Heights*, https://www.niagarafallsinfo.com/niagara-falls-history/niagara-falls-municipal-history/the-war-of-1812/the-battle-of-queenston-heights/ , accessed 4-20-22.

83. *Noah Webster Reforms the Teaching of English in the United States*, Jerry Norman's History Information.com, 3-6-2020, https://www.historyofinformation.com/detail.php?id=3228.

84. Noll, Mark A., *America's God: From Jonathan Edwards to Abraham Lincoln*, Oxford University Press, Oct 3, 2002.

85. North's Gazetteer of Genesee County 1899.

86. North, Safford E, *Our County and Its People; A Descriptive and Biographical Record of Genesee County, New York*, [Boston: Boston History Company, 1899], Cornell Americana, Cornell University, https://archive.org/details/cu31924028853450/page/n89/mode/2up?q=daniel+davis.

87. Olson, Albert Laverne, *"Agricultural Economy and the Population in Eighteenth-Century Connecticut"*, Published for the Tercentenary Commission by the Yale University Press, 1935.

88. Parker, Arthur C., *"The Senecas in the War of 1812."*, Proceedings of the New York State Historical Association, 1916, Vol. 15 (1916), pp. 78-90 Published by: Fenimore Art Museum Stable URL: https://www.jstor.org/stable/4288952

89. Petruzzello, Melissa, ed., *Second Great Awakening*, Britannica, https://www.britannica.com/topic/Second-Great-Awakening, accessed 3-18-2022.

90. Perry, Peg, *The War of 1812: European Traces in a British-American Conflict*, Lithuanian Museum-Archives of Canada December 28, 2020,

https://www.lithuanianheritage.ca/wp-content/uploads/2021/04/KLMA-LMAC-War-of-1812-12-28-2020.pdf, accessed 5-24-22.

91. *Philip Syng Physick, 1768-1837*, Penn People, University Archives, University of Pennsylvania, https://archives.upenn.edu/exhibits/penn-people/biography/philip-syng-physick/, accessed 5-7-2022.

92. *"Population of New York by Counties"*, https://ocgov.net/sites/default/files/planning/PlanPages/censustables/nyshist17902000.pdf

93. Presentation Sword and Scabbard of Brigadier General Daniel Davis (1777–1814) of the New York Militia ca. 1815–17, The Met, John Targee American, https://www.metmuseum.org/art/collection/search/22769

94. Prom, William J., *The U.S. Navy in the War of 1812: Winning the Battle, but Losing the War*, Center for International Maritime Security, Nov. 18, 2019, https://cimsec.org/the-u-s-navy-in-the-war-of-1812-winning-the-battle-but-losing-the-war-pt-1/, accessed 4-23-2022.

95. Pruitt, Sarah, *"13 Everyday Objects of Colonial America, History"*, 2022 A&E Television Networks, LLC.

96. Purvis, Thomas *"Colonial America to 1763. Facts On File Inc."*, 199, p. 54.

97. Robertson, John K., "*Decoding Connecticut Militia 1739-1783*", Journal of the American Revolution, July 27, 2016, 3-5-2022, Decoding Connecticut Militia 1739-1783 - Journal of the American Revolution (allthingsliberty.com)

98. *Record of service of Connecticut men in the I. War of the Revolution, II. War of 1812, III. Mexican War:* Connecticut. Adjutant-General's Office, Connecticut Military record 1775-1848, Hartford, 1889.

99. Rootsweb, trees4u, 05-05-2019 16:05:13. Owner: Barbara, https://wc.rootsweb.com/trees/235320/I12169/solomon-davis/individual

100. Samson, John P., *History of Brigadier Daniel Davis*, compiled from local sources, 1929.

101. Sawyer, William, National Park Ranger Fort Stanwix National Park, NY, "The Six Nations Confederacy During the American Revolution", https://www.nps.gov/fost/learn/historyculture/the-six-nations-confederacy-during-the-american-revolution.htm#CP_JUMP_3550115.

102. Schenawolf, Harry, "*Gunpowder and its Supply in the American Revolutionary War*", Revolutionary War Journal, November 30, 2014, https://www.revolutionarywarjournal.com/gunpowder/, accessed 3-1-2022.

103. Schuman, Michael, "*History of child labor in the United States—part 1: little children working,*" Monthly Labor Review, U.S. Bureau of Labor Statistics, January,

2017, https://doi.org/10.21916/mlr.2017.1, accessed 3-8-2022.

104. Scott, Winfield, *Memoirs of Lieut.-General Winfield Scott, LL.-D., Vol. 1,* New York, Sheldon and Company Publishers, 1864.

105. Seneca Indian Country Historical Marker (hmdb.org) LeRoy, New York.

106. Siles, William Herbert, "A Vision of Wealth Speculators and Settlers in the Genesee Country of New York 1798-1800.", A dissertation for PhD History, UMASS, May 1978. https://core.ac.uk/download/pdf/32438474.pdf, accessed 3-28-2022.

107. Silsby, Robert, "The Holland Land Company in Western New York", The Holland Land Company in Western New York.pdf (nylearns.org). accessed 3-13-2022.

108. Skeen, C. Edward, *Citizen Soldiers in the War of 1812,* University of Press of Kentucky, 2021. https://www.google.com/books/edition/Citizen_Soldiers_in_the_War_of_1812/u-MzEAAAQBAJ?hl=en&gbpv=1&dq=brigadier+general+daniel+davis+war+of+1812&pg=PT167&printsec=frontcover, accessed 5-11-2022.

109. Smith, Mary, E., "A History of the Early Development of the Towns of LeRoy, Bergen, Sweden, Clarkson and Hamlin New York" (1984). Local History Books. Book 19. http://digitalcommons.brockport.edu/local_books/19.

110. Strum, Harvey. "New York Federalists and Opposition to the War of 1812." *World Affairs* 142, no. 3 (1980): 169–87. http://www.jstor.org/stable/20671825.

111. Strum, H. (2020). New York Militia and Opposition to the War of 1812. *New York History 101*(1), 114-132. doi:10.1353/nyh.2020.0008.

112. Tabbert, Mark, *"FreemasonryinColonialAmerica"*, https://www.mountvernon.org/george-washington/freemasonry/freemasonry-in-colonial-america/

113. The War of 1812 - (Siege of Fort Erie) (theuswarof1812.org)

114. "The Growth of the Colonies", Boundless US History (lumenlearning.com) accessed 2-19-2022.

115. *"The Importance of Being Puritan: Church and State in Colonial Connecticut"*, Connecticut History, a CTHumanities *Project*, accessed 2-19-2020.

116. *"The Oldest US Newspaper in Continuous Publication"*, https://connecticuthistory.org/the-oldest-newspaper-in-continuous-publication/, accessed 2-26-2022.

117. Tompkins, Daniel D., Public Papers of Daniel D. Tompkins, Governor of New York, 1807- 1817, Volume 3.

118. *"Town of LeRoy"*, William G. Pomeroy Foundation (wgpfoundation.org), accessed 4-26-2022.

119. Townshend, Charles, Hervey, *The British Invasion of New Haven, Connecticut, Together with Some Account of Their Landing and Burning The Towns of Fairfield and Norwalk, July 1779.*, Tuttle, Morehouse, and Taylor, 1879.

120. Tufts, Aaron, *"Some Reminisces from the Past"*, LeRoy Gazette, 9-21-1859.

121. Turner, O., *History of the Pioneer Settlement of Phelps and Gorman's Purchase and Morris Reserve*, Published by William Alling, Rochester, 1851.

122. *"United States, New York Land Records, 1630-1975"*, *Index of Deeds Genesee County*, database with images, 183FamilySearch (https://www.familysearch.org/ark:/61903/1:1:CGR7-52T2: 3 March 2021), Daniel Davis, 1805.

123. Volo, James M. PhD., Contributor/Ed of Encyclopedias ofHistory(1998-present),Quora, https://www.quora.com/How-many-acres-could-a-family-farm-manage-in-the-18th-century-thirteen-colonies?q=How%20many%20acres%20was%20in%20the%20typical%20size%20of%20a%20%20farm%20in%2018th%20century%20New%20England%3F, accessed 3-20-2022.

124. War-of-1812-panels-for-web.pdf (historicgeneva.org)

125. *"War of 1812 Timeline"*, National Society of Daughters of War of 1812, https://usdaughters1812.org/war-of-1812-timeline-mobile/, accessed 4-24-2022.

126. Whitehorne, Joseph, *While Wahington Burned: The Battle for Fort Erie*, The Nautical and Aviation Publishing Company of America Incorporated, 1992.

127. *"Who Was Lorenzo Dow?"*, Signpost, Volume 17, Issue 5, February 2007, Coventry Historical Society, https://view.officeapps.live.com/op/view.aspx?src=https%3A%2F%2Fctcoventryhistoricalsociety.dreamhoste

rs.com%2Fwp-content%2Fuploads%2F2019%2F05%2FSignpost-February-07.doc&wdOrigin=BROWSELINK.,accessed 3-18-2022.

128. Wigger, John H., *"Holy Knock'em Down Preachers",* Chrisitan History,No.45,1995, https://christianhistoryinstitute.org/magazine/article/knock-em-down-preachers, accessed 3-24-2022.

129. Wigger, John H., *Taking Heaven by Storm, Methodism and the Rise of Popular Christianity in America,*

130. Worthington, *Nathan Starr 1812 Contract Calvary Saber.*

131. Worthington Galleries, Nathan Starr Model 1812 Contract Calvary Saber – Used in War of 1812 , Worthington GalleriesPart1, https://worthingtongalleries.com/shop/american-civil-war-2/nathan-starr-model-1812-contract-calvary-saber-used-in-war-of-1812/#:~:text=The%20leading%20sword%20maker%20in,Starr%20contract%20of%201812-1813.

132. Wright, Robert E. *One Nation Under Debt: Hamilton, Jefferson, and the History of What We Owe.* New York: McGraw-Hill, 2008.

www.ingramcontent.com/pod-product-compliance
Lightning Source LLC
Chambersburg PA
CBHW072015070526
44583CB00015B/1489